ECONOMIC ISSUES, PROBLEMS AND PERSPECTIVES

AF760860

THE FAIR LABOR STANDARDS ACT AND NATIONAL LABOR RELATIONS ACT

ECONOMIC ISSUES, PROBLEMS AND PERSPECTIVES

Additional books in this series can be found on Nova's website under the Series tab.

Additional E-books in this series can be found on Nova's website under the E-book tab.

AMERICA IN THE 21ST CENTURY: POLITICAL AND ECONOMIC ISSUES

Additional books in this series can be found on Nova's website under the Series tab.

Additional E-books in this series can be found on Nova's website under the E-book tab.

ECONOMIC ISSUES, PROBLEMS AND PERSPECTIVES

THE FAIR LABOR STANDARDS ACT AND NATIONAL LABOR RELATIONS ACT

JULIAN A. SOTELO
EDITOR

NOVINKA

New York

Library of Congress Cataloging-in-Publication Data

ISBN: 978-1-62808-301-9

Published by Nova Science Publishers, Inc. † New York

CONTENTS

PREFACE

The Fair Labor Standards Act (FLSA) provides workers with minimum wage, overtime pay, and child labor protections. The FLSA covers most, but not all, private and public sector employees. In addition, certain employers and employees are exempt from coverage. Provisions of the FLSA that are of current interest to Congress include the basic minimum wage, subminimum wage rates, exemptions from overtime and the minimum wage for persons who provide companionship services, the exemption for employees in computer-related occupations, compensatory time in lieu of overtime pay, and break time for nursing mothers. The National Labor Relations Act (NLRA) recognizes the right of employees to engage in collective bargaining through representatives of their own choosing. By "encouraging the practice and procedure of collective bargaining," the Act attempts to mitigate and eliminate labor-related obstructions to the free flow of commerce. Although union membership has declined dramatically since the 1950s, congressional interest in the NLRA remains significant. This book provides an overview of both the Fair Labor Standards Act and the National Labor Relations Act with a focus on coverage, amendments and policy.

Chapter 1 - The Fair Labor Standards Act (FLSA) provides workers with minimum wage, overtime pay, and child labor protections. The FLSA covers most, but not all, private and public sector employees. In addition, certain employers and employees are exempt from coverage.

Provisions of the FLSA that are of current interest to Congress include the basic minimum wage, subminimum wage rates, exemptions from overtime and the minimum wage for persons who provide companionship services, the exemption for employees in computer-related occupations, compensatory time ("comp time") in lieu of overtime pay, and break time for nursing mothers.

Basic Minimum Wage

- The FLSA requires employers to pay covered, nonexempt employees at least the minimum wage. In 2007, the basic minimum wage was raised, in steps, from $5.15 to $7.25 an hour. The basic minimum wage was raised to $7.25 an hour effective July 24, 2009. As of January 1, 2013, 19 states and the District of Columbia have minimum wage rates that are higher than the federal minimum wage rate.
- Basic minimum wage rates in American Samoa and the Commonwealth of the Northern Mariana Islands (CNMI) are lower than in the continental United States. In 2007, Congress passed the Fair Minimum Wage Act of 2007 (P.L. 110- 28), which mandated annual increases of $0.50 an hour in the minimum wages of American Samoa and CNMI. In 2010, Congress temporarily suspended these increases. The minimum wage in CNMI increased by $0.50 an hour to $5.55 on September 30, 2012. In July 2012, Congress delayed the increases in American Samoa. The next minimum wage increases in American Samoa are scheduled for September 30, 2015.

Subminimum Wage Rates

- Tipped employees may be paid less than the basic minimum wage, but their cash wage plus tips must equal at least the basic minimum wage of $7.25. Employers may pay tipped workers $2.13 an hour in cash wages, provided the employees receive at least $5.12 an hour in tips. The latter amount is called a "tip credit."
- Employers may pay special minimum wages (SMWs) to workers with disabilities. The purpose of the SMWs is to provide persons with disabilities the opportunity to work.

Overtime

- The FLSA requires employers to pay at least time-and-a-half to covered, nonexempt employees who work more than 40 hours in a week at a given job.

The FLSA allows covered, nonexempt state and local government employees to receive compensatory time off (comp time) for hours worked over 40 in a workweek. Comp time is time off with pay in lieu of overtime pay.

Exemptions

- The FLSA exempts certain employers and employees from the minimum wage, overtime pay, or child labor standards of the act.
- Certain employees in computer-related occupations are exempt from both the minimum wage and overtime standards of the FLSA if they meet an hourly wage or weekly salary test and a job duties test.

Domestic service workers who provide companionship services in private homes are exempt from both the minimum wage and overtime requirements of the FLSA. Under regulations proposed by the U.S. Department of Labor (DOL), minimum wage and overtime coverage would be extended to companions employed by a third party. Overtime pay would be extended to live-in domestic service workers employed by a third party.

Chapter 2 - The Fair Labor Standards Act (FLSA) sets minimum standards for hourly wages, overtime pay, and child labor. The FLSA requires employers to pay covered employees at least $7.25 an hour and at least one-and-a-half times their regular hourly wage for hours worked over 40 hours a week at a given job. However, the FLSA includes a number of exemptions that exclude certain employees from the minimum wage and overtime standards of the act.

Section 13(a)(1) of the FLSA exempts from both the minimum wage and overtime pay standards of the act any person who is employed in a bona fide executive, administrative, or professional occupation (the EAP exemption). Before 1990, employees in computer-related occupations were exempt if they met the requirements of the EAP exemption.

In 1990, Congress directed the Secretary of Labor to issue regulations that would allow "computer systems analysts, computer programmers, software engineers, and other similarly skilled professional workers" to qualify as exempt executive, administrative, or professional employees under Section 13(a)(1) of the FLSA. The 1990 legislation also directed Congress to apply the EAP exemption to employees in computer-related occupations if they were paid on an hourly basis at a rate of at least six-and-a-half times the basic federal minimum wage. At the time, the federal minimum wage was $4.25 an hour. Thus, hourly computer employees were exempt if they met the job duties test and were paid at least $27.63 an hour. In 1992, the U.S. Department of Labor (DOL) published a final rule that implemented the 1990 legislation. The regulations treated computer employees as professional employees under the EAP exemption.

In 1996, Congress amended the FLSA to add a specific exemption for computer employees. The amendments fixed the minimum hourly wage for computer professionals at $27.63 an hour and included in statute much of the regulatory language from the 1992 regulations that defined the primary duties of computer professionals.

In 2004, DOL issued new regulations that revised the salary and duties tests for the EAP exemption. The regulations also simplified the duties test for computer professionals to reflect the 1996 amendments to the FLSA. Under the 2004 regulations, whether they are paid by the hour (at a minimum rate of $27.63) or the week (at a minimum rate of $455), computer professionals are exempt from the minimum wage and overtime standards of the FLSA if they meet the job duties test provided in regulations.

Employees in certain computer-related occupations are not exempt and must be paid at least the minimum wage and time-and-a-half for overtime. The exemption for workers in computer occupations does not include employees engaged in the manufacture or repair of computer hardware. Employees whose work is highly dependent on the use of computers but who are not engaged primarily in computer systems analysis, programming, or other similarly skilled computer occupations are not exempt. Depending on their job duties, Information Technology (IT) Support Specialists may not be exempt from the minimum wage and overtime standards of the FLSA.

In recent Congresses, legislation has been introduced that would expand the statutory exemption for computer employees to include workers whose job duties include network or database analysis and workers who manage or train employees who qualify for the exemption.

Chapter 3 - The National Labor Relations Act (NLRA or "the Act") recognizes the right of employees to engage in collective bargaining through representatives of their own choosing. By "encouraging the practice and procedure of collective bargaining," the Act attempts to mitigate and eliminate labor-related obstructions to the free flow of commerce. Although union membership has declined dramatically since the 1950s, congressional interest in the NLRA remains significant. In the 112th Congress, over 30 bills have been introduced to amend the NLRA. Some of these bills address the timing of union representation elections, while others are concerned with varying aspects of the NLRA, such as the activities of the National Labor Relations Board (NLRB), which implements and administers the Act.

Since the NLRA's enactment in 1935, the NLRB and the courts have considered a variety of issues arising under the Act. This report reviews selected decisions of the NLRB and the courts on three of them. Determining when an employee may be deemed a supervisor for purposes of coverage under the Act is important because the right to engage in collective bargaining is extended only to employees under the NLRA. Employees who are properly classified as supervisors are not afforded collective bargaining rights.

Both employers and unions are prohibited from restraining or coercing employees in the exercise of the rights guaranteed to them under the Act. In general, to determine whether an unfair labor practice has been committed by either an employer or union, a reviewing court asks whether the misconduct "reasonably tends" to restrain or coerce employees in the exercise of their rights under the NLRA. Courts have emphasized that the actual effect of the misconduct is immaterial.

Finally, pre-election communication with employees may influence the outcome of a representation election. While the NLRA does prohibit an employer from interfering with an employee's collective bargaining rights, decisions discussed in this report indicate that an employer does not violate the Act in all cases when it denies a union access to its property.

Chapter 4 - The National Labor Relations Act (NLRA) establishes certain protections for private sector employees who want to form or join a labor union. These protections do not extend to supervisors. Historically, Congress has debated where to draw the line between employees who have different levels of management responsibility. It is generally agreed that employees who have significant supervisory duties, such as hiring and firing, are supervisors. However, disagreement occurs with respect to employees who have minor supervisory duties.

In 2001, the U.S. Supreme Court ruled that the test administered by the National Labor Relations Board ("NLRB" or the "Board") to determine whether an employee is a supervisor was inconsistent with the NLRA. In response to *NLRB v. Kentucky River Community Care, Inc.*, the Board issued a September 2006 decision in *Oakwood Healthcare, Inc.* in which it established new definitions for three key terms that are used to identify supervisors for purposes of the NLRA: to "assign" and "responsibly to direct" employees and to exercise "independent judgment."

Applying the new definitions, the NLRB concluded that 12 permanent charge nurses employed by Oakwood Healthcare were supervisors. The Board found that the nurses exercised independent judgment in assigning employees to patients and assigning overall tasks to other employees. However, the Board found that none of the charge nurses at Oakwood Healthcare responsibly directed other employees.

In the 112th Congress, Senator Richard Blumenthal introduced the Re-Empowerment of Skilled and Professional Employees and Construction Tradesworkers (RESPECT) Act (S. 2168). The legislation was also introduced in the 110th Congress by Representative Robert Andrews and Senator Chris Dodd (H.R. 1644/S. 969).

The RESPECT Act would narrow the definition of the term "supervisor" in the NLRA. The legislation would eliminate "assign" and "responsibly to direct" from the current definition of supervisor in the NLRA. In addition, the act would add a limiting phrase to the definition of supervisor. Under the act, employees would be classified as supervisors if they are engaged in supervisory activities more than 50% of the time. Currently, an employee may be classified as a supervisor if the employee acts as a supervisor for at least 10%-15% of the employee's worktime. This change would reduce the number of employees who are classified as supervisors and, therefore, increase the number of employees protected by the NLRA.

The RESPECT Act, if it were enacted, may have a significant impact on foremen. In 1947, the Supreme Court upheld the position that the Board followed at the time that supervisors were included in the definition of employee. In response, Congress amended the NLRA to exclude supervisors from the definition of employee. The new definition was included in the Labor Management Relations Act of 1947 (P.L. 80-101). Because the RESPECT Act would eliminate "responsibly to direct" as a supervisory function, foremen and employees with similar duties may no longer be classified as supervisors. They could, therefore, receive the same protections as other employees under the NLRA.

In: The Fair Labor Standards Act …
Editor: Julian A. Sotelo
ISBN: 978-1-62808-301-9

Chapter 1

THE FAIR LABOR STANDARDS ACT (FLSA): AN OVERVIEW*

Gerald Mayer, Benjamin Collins and David H. Bradley

SUMMARY

The Fair Labor Standards Act (FLSA) provides workers with minimum wage, overtime pay, and child labor protections. The FLSA covers most, but not all, private and public sector employees. In addition, certain employers and employees are exempt from coverage.

Provisions of the FLSA that are of current interest to Congress include the basic minimum wage, subminimum wage rates, exemptions from overtime and the minimum wage for persons who provide companionship services, the exemption for employees in computer-related occupations, compensatory time ("comp time") in lieu of overtime pay, and break time for nursing mothers.

Basic Minimum Wage

- The FLSA requires employers to pay covered, nonexempt employees at least the minimum wage. In 2007, the basic minimum wage was raised, in steps, from $5.15 to $7.25 an hour. The basic minimum wage was raised to $7.25 an hour effective

---

* This is an edited, reformatted and augmented version of a Congressional Research Service publication, CRS Report for Congress R42713, prepared for Members and Committees of Congress, from www.crs.gov, dated May 3, 2013.

July 24, 2009. As of January 1, 2013, 19 states and the District of Columbia have minimum wage rates that are higher than the federal minimum wage rate.

- Basic minimum wage rates in American Samoa and the Commonwealth of the Northern Mariana Islands (CNMI) are lower than in the continental United States. In 2007, Congress passed the Fair Minimum Wage Act of 2007 (P.L. 110- 28), which mandated annual increases of $0.50 an hour in the minimum wages of American Samoa and CNMI. In 2010, Congress temporarily suspended these increases. The minimum wage in CNMI increased by $0.50 an hour to $5.55 on September 30, 2012. In July 2012, Congress delayed the increases in American Samoa. The next minimum wage increases in American Samoa are scheduled for September 30, 2015.

Subminimum Wage Rates

- Tipped employees may be paid less than the basic minimum wage, but their cash wage plus tips must equal at least the basic minimum wage of $7.25. Employers may pay tipped workers $2.13 an hour in cash wages, provided the employees receive at least $5.12 an hour in tips. The latter amount is called a "tip credit."
- Employers may pay special minimum wages (SMWs) to workers with disabilities. The purpose of the SMWs is to provide persons with disabilities the opportunity to work.

Overtime

- The FLSA requires employers to pay at least time-and-a-half to covered, nonexempt employees who work more than 40 hours in a week at a given job.

The FLSA allows covered, nonexempt state and local government employees to receive compensatory time off (comp time) for hours worked over 40 in a workweek. Comp time is time off with pay in lieu of overtime pay.

Exemptions

- The FLSA exempts certain employers and employees from the minimum wage, overtime pay, or child labor standards of the act.
- Certain employees in computer-related occupations are exempt from both the minimum wage and overtime standards of the

FLSA if they meet an hourly wage or weekly salary test and a job duties test.

Domestic service workers who provide companionship services in private homes are exempt from both the minimum wage and overtime requirements of the FLSA. Under regulations proposed by the U.S. Department of Labor (DOL), minimum wage and overtime coverage would be extended to companions employed by a third party. Overtime pay would be extended to live-in domestic service workers employed by a third party.

INTRODUCTION

In 1937, the United States was recovering from the Great Depression. As part of the recovery effort, President Franklin D. Roosevelt endorsed a series of economic programs, known as the New Deal, to help stimulate and rebuild the U.S. economy. The National Industrial Recovery Act (NIRA) was the major statute enacted to help achieve these goals. Although the NIRA was eventually found unconstitutional, many of its provisions appeared in later New Deal statutes, including in the Fair Labor Standards Act of 1938 (FLSA).[1]

WORKING FAMILIES FLEXIBILITY ACT OF 2013

On April 9, 2013, Representative Martha Roby introduced H.R. 1406, the Working Families Flexibility Act of 2013. The Subcommittee on Workforce Protections of the House Committee on Education and the Workforce held a hearing on the bill on April 11, 2013.

The full committee favorably reported the bill, as amended, to the House on April 30, 2013.

The FLSA requires employers to pay covered, nonexempt workers at least one-and-a-half times their regular hourly wage for hours worked in excess of 40 hours in a week. H.R. 1406 would amend the FLSA to allow private sector employers to offer employees compensatory time off (i.e., "comp" time) in place of overtime pay. Employees would receive at least one and a half hours of paid comp time for each hour of overtime worked.

The use of comp time would be optional for both employers and employees. Employers could provide comp time to employees under the provisions of a collective bargaining agreement or under an agreement between an employer and employee. An employee could choose to accept or reject an offer of comp time. An employee may withdraw from a comp time agreement at any time. An employer may withdraw from a comp time agreement with 30 days notice.

Employees would be eligible for comp time if they have worked at least 1,000 hours for their employer in a period of continuous employment in the year before agreeing to or receiving comp time. Employees could accumulate up to 160 hours of comp time. An employee who requests to use comp time would be permitted to take time off within "a reasonable period" after making the request if the use of comp time does not "unduly disrupt" the employer's operations.

Under the act, several circumstances would trigger the conversion of accrued comp time into a monetary payment:

- At the end of each calendar year (or at the conclusion of another specified 12- month period), an employer must provide monetary compensation for any unused comp time.
- An employee may request accrued comp time to be converted to monetary payment at any time. The employer must comply with this request within 30 days.
- An employer, with 30 days notice, may convert any accrued comp time in excess of 80 hours to a monetary payment.
- If employment is terminated, either voluntarily or involuntarily, accrued comp time must be converted to a monetary payment.

When comp time is converted to a monetary payment, the rate of compensation shall be the higher of (1) the regular rate received by the employee when the comp time was earned or (2) the final regular rate received by the employee.

Under the act, an employer that provides comp time could not intimidate, threaten, or coerce any employee to use comp time or interfere with an employee's right to request or refuse comp time. An employer who violates this provision would be required to pay the employee for the amount of comp time earned plus an equal amount in damages.

The amendments made to the FLSA by H.R. 1406 would expire five years after the date of enactment of the act.

THE FAIR LABOR STANDARDS ACT[2]

The FLSA provides for a federal minimum wage, overtime pay, and child labor protections. Congress endorsed the act because its provisions were meant to both protect workers and stimulate the economy. The FLSA also created the Wage and Hour Division (WHD) within the Department of Labor (DOL) to administer and enforce the act.[3]

At the time of the act's passage, Congress found that a few employers who paid substandard wages caused a decrease in wages within their respective industries, because other employers sought to compete in the marketplace with lower priced goods.[4] Congress also found that these decreased wages caused one-third of the U.S. population to be "ill-nourished, ill-clad, and illhoused."[5] To counter these conditions, in 1938 Congress established a minimum wage of $0.25 an hour, gradually increasing to $0.40 an hour in 1945.[6] Congress has since legislated several increases in the minimum wage. It now stands at $7.25 an hour.

The FLSA also mandates a pay rate of one-and-one-half times an employee's hourly wage for every hour the employee works beyond a standard work week. When enacted, the FLSA required employers to pay overtime for hours worked in excess of 44 hours in a week.[7] The 44-hour threshold was lowered to 40 hours in 1940. The purpose of the overtime provision is to reduce unemployment by encouraging employers to hire more workers, rather than requiring current employees to work more than 40 hours per week and pay the premium overtime rate.

Finally, under the FLSA Congress set certain conditions under which children could work. Not only was oppressive child labor considered immoral, as children often worked at the cost of their own health and education, but Congress also believed that the lower wages generally earned by children drove down the wages of adult workers.[8]

The FLSA extends minimum wage, overtime pay, and child labor protections to individuals "employed by an employer."[9] Congress has also "exempted" certain employers and employees from all or parts of the FLSA. For example, exemptions were provided to executive, administrative, or professional (EAP) employees; individuals employed at retail stores that did not have interstate operations, and agricultural employees. Additionally, the child labor provisions did not apply to children employed in the motion picture or theater industries.[10]

WHO IS COVERED BY THE FLSA?

The FLSA covers employees and enterprises engaged in interstate commerce. An enterprise is covered if it has annual sales or business done of at least $500,000.[11] Regardless of the dollar volume of business, the act applies to hospitals; institutions primarily engaged in the care of the sick, aged, mentally ill, or disabled who reside on the premises; schools for children who are mentally or physically disabled or gifted; federal, state, and local governments; and preschools, elementary and secondary schools, and institutions of higher education.[12]

Although enterprises that have *less than* $500,000 in annual sales or business done are not covered by the FLSA, employees of these enterprises may be covered if they are individually engaged in interstate commerce. These employees may travel to other states for work, make phone calls or send emails to persons in other states, or handle records that are involved in interstate transactions.[13]

The $500,000 enterprise threshold has not been raised since it was enacted in 1989. Employers are required to administer dual enterprise and individual tests to determine if individual employees are covered by the act. That is, although an enterprise may not be covered if it has less than $500,000 in annual sales or business done, employees of the enterprise may be covered if they are individually engaged in interstate commerce.

The FLSA covers most, but not all, private and public sector employees. Persons who are not covered by the FLSA include individuals who are elected to state or local government offices and members of their staffs, policymaking appointees of elected officeholders of state or local governments, employees of legislative bodies of state or local governments, immediate family members of an employer engaged in agriculture, persons who volunteer their services to a state or local government (if the person is not employed by the government agency to perform the same services), and persons who volunteer their services to a private, nonprofit food bank and who receive groceries from the food bank.[14]

The FLSA exempts certain employers and employees from the minimum wage, overtime, or child labor standards of the act. For example, bona fide executive, administrative, and professional employees are exempt from both overtime and the minimum wage if they meet both a salary test and a job duties test. Certain employees in computer-related occupations are also exempt from both overtime and the minimum wage if they meet an hourly wage or weekly salary test and a job duties test. Domestic service workers who provide companionship services in private homes are exempt from both overtime and the minimum wage.

RELATION OF THE FLSA TO STATE LAWS

Under Section 18 of the FLSA, if states enact minimum wage, overtime, or child labor laws that are more protective of employees than what is provided by the FLSA, the state law applies. The FLSA defines a state as "any State of the United States or the District of Columbia or any Territory or possession of the United States."[15]

Because states may enact laws that are more protective of employees than what is provided by the FLSA, there are multiple minimum wage, overtime, and child labor standards nationwide.

MINIMUM WAGE RATES

Under Section 6 of the FLSA, employers must pay covered, nonexempt employees at least $7.25 an hour.[16] However, the FLSA includes several subminimum wage rates. Employers may pay lower minimum wage rates to tipped employees; workers with disabilities; new hires under the age of 20; full-time students who work in retail or service establishments, agriculture, or institutions of higher education; and high school students who are at least 16 years of age and enrolled in a vocational education program.

The Basic Minimum Wage

The basic minimum wage is raised periodically by Congress. The current basic minimum wage of $7.25 went into effect on July 24, 2009.[17] As of January 1, 2013, 19 states and the District of Columbia have minimum wage rates that are higher than the federal minimum wage.[18]

Most employees are paid more than the basic minimum wage. According to the Bureau of Labor Statistics (BLS), in 2011 94.8% of employees who were paid by the hour were paid an hourly wage that was greater than the federal minimum wage of $7.25.[19]

Tipped Workers

Tipped employees may be paid less than the basic minimum wage, but their cash wage plus tips must equal at least the basic minimum wage.

Under Section 3(m) of the FLSA, a "tipped employee" is a worker who "customarily and regularly" receives more than $30 a month in tips. Employers must allow tipped employees to keep all tips. However, the FLSA allows tips to be pooled and shared among tipped employees.

Under the FLSA, an employer may pay a tipped worker a minimum cash wage of $2.13 if the employee receives at least $5.12 an hour in tips (for a total hourly wage of $7.25).[20] Employers may claim up to $5.12 in tips as a tip credit. However, if a tipped employee receives less than $5.12 an hour in tips, the employer must make up the difference with a higher cash wage. For example, if a tipped employee receives $3.00 an hour in tips, the employer must pay the employee a cash wage of at least $4.25 an hour.

In states with a minimum wage that is higher than the federal minimum wage, the tip credit may be more than $5.12. On the other hand, as of January 1, 2012, seven states and Guam do not allow employers to claim a tip credit (i.e., employers must pay all tipped employees a cash wage that is at least the higher of the federal or state minimum wage). In 24 states and the District of Columbia, the minimum cash wage for tipped employees is greater than the federal minimum cash wage of $2.13. In 13 states and the Virgin Islands, the minimum cash wage for tipped employees is $2.13. In the remaining six states, five do not have state minimum wage laws and one exempts tipped employees from state law.[21]

Workers with Disabilities

Under Section 14(c) of the FLSA, employers may pay special minimum wages (SMWs) to workers with disabilities. The purpose of the SMWs is to provide persons with disabilities the opportunity to work. A disability may be physical or mental. It may be related to age or an injury. Disabilities include blindness, mental illness or retardation, alcoholism, and drug addiction.[22]

Employers must receive certificates from the Wage and Hour Division (WHD) of DOL that authorize the employers to pay SMWs.[23] WHD issues certificates to four types of employers: work centers, hospital or residential care facilities, businesses, and School Work Exploration Programs (SWEP). Work centers (also called "community rehabilitation programs" and "sheltered workshops") provide employment, training, and rehabilitation services. Hospital or residential care facilities employ "patient workers," who are employed persons who also receive treatment or care. A business establishment that employs workers with disabilities at SMWs must receive a certificate from WHD. Under SWEP, schools place students with disabilities at work sites in the community.

In order to pay a disabled worker less than the basic minimum wage, the employee's disabilities must impair his or her productive capacity in the job being performed. The wages paid must be "commensurate" to the worker's productivity. The worker's wage must be based on the worker's productivity relative to the wages and productivity of experienced workers who are not disabled and who perform the same type and quality of work in the same geographic area. For disabled workers paid an hourly wage, employers must review the workers' productivity, and adjust their wages accordingly, at least every six months. The wages of all disabled workers must also be adjusted at least once a year to take into account changes in wages paid to experienced, nondisabled workers.[24]

An employee paid a SMW, or the employee's parent or guardian, may ask WHD to review the wage paid to the employee.

New Hires Under the Age of 20

Under what is known as the "youth opportunity wage," employers may pay a minimum wage of $4.25 an hour to employees under the age of 20 for their first 90 consecutive calendar days of employment.[25] Hiring youth at a subminimum wage cannot displace other workers. After 90 consecutive days of employment or when the worker reaches age 20, whichever comes first, the employee must be paid at least the basic minimum wage.

The purpose of the youth subminimum wage is to provide employment opportunities to young persons, especially disadvantaged youth. Some policymakers question whether it is appropriate to pay subminimum wage rates to persons under 20, especially if they have held other jobs.

Full-Time Students

Under Section 14(b) of the FLSA, employers may pay certain full-time students 85% of the basic minimum wage. The subminimum wage for full-time students applies to students employed by retail or service stores, in agriculture, or by institutions of higher education. Again, the purpose of the subminimum wage for full-time students is to provide these students with opportunities for employment. The FLSA does not impose an age limit on the subminimum wage for full-time students.

Student Learners

Under Section 14(a) of the FLSA, employers may pay "student learners" 75% of the basic minimum wage. Student learners are high school students who are (1) at least 16 years old (or 18 if employed in an occupation that the Secretary of Labor has declared to be particularly hazardous for the employment of youth), (2) are receiving instruction in an accredited school, college, or university, and (3) are employed part-time by an employer as part of a vocational training program. The employer may pay student learners a subminimum wage for as long as the students are enrolled in the vocational education program. Employers must obtain certificates from DOL authorizing them to pay less than the basic minimum wage.[26]

Minimum Wage Rates in the Territories and Possessions of the United States

When the FLSA was enacted in 1938, the minimum wage in Guam, Puerto Rico, and the Virgin Islands was set at the same rate as in the continental United States ($0.25 an hour).[27] The minimum wage that applies in the continental United States has applied to Guam since 1938. However, in 1940 Congress enacted legislation that allowed Special Industry Committees (SICs) to set minimum wage rates by industry in Puerto Rico and the Virgin Islands. In 1989, Congress enacted legislation that eliminated the SIC structure in both territories. The minimum wage in the Virgin Islands has been the same as in the continental United States since 1989. In Puerto Rico, minimum wages by industry were raised, in steps, until they were the same as in the continental United States by April 1, 1996.

American Samoa and the Commonwealth of the Northern Mariana Islands (CNMI) were not covered by the FLSA of 1938. In 1956, Congress enacted legislation that required the Secretary of Labor to establish minimum wages in American Samoa based on recommendations from SICs. In 2007, Congress passed the Fair Minimum Wage Act of 2007 (P.L. 110-28).[28] For American Samoa, the act mandated annual increases of $0.50 an hour until the minimum wage in each industry reached the federal minimum wage. However, in 2010 Congress passed legislation (P.L. 111-244) that postponed the planned increases for 2010 and 2011.[29] In July 2012, Congress passed, and the President signed, the Insular Areas Act of 2011 (P.L. 112-149). The act delayed the increases in the minimum wages in American Samoa for 2012, 2013, and 2014. The next minimum wage increases in American Samoa are scheduled for September 30, 2015. Thereafter, increases will be made every three years until they reach the federal minimum wage.

In the mid-1970s, the United States and CNMI entered into a Covenant of Association. CNMI retained control over the minimum wage in the islands. However, as was the case with American Samoa, P.L. 110-28 mandated that the minimum wage in CNMI be raised by $0.50 a year until it reached the same level as in the continental United States. However, P.L. 111-244 postponed the scheduled increase in the minimum wage for 2011. On September 30, 2012, the minimum wage in CNMI increased by $0.50 an hour to $5.55.

OVERTIME

Under Section 7, employers must pay covered workers at least one-and-a-half times their regular hourly wage for hours worked over 40 hours a week at a given job. Employers may choose to pay more than time-and-a-half for overtime or to pay overtime to employees who are exempt from overtime under the FLSA. Under the FLSA, overtime pay applies to hours worked in excess of 40 in a workweek. Thus, the law allows some flexibility in work hours. For example, an employer could schedule four 10-hour workdays in a workweek without asking employees to work overtime. Similarly, an employee who works a five-day workweek could work four hours one day and nine hours the other four days and not work overtime.[30]

Comp Time in Lieu of Overtime Pay

The FLSA, under Section 7(o), allows covered, nonexempt state and local government employees to receive compensatory time off ("comp time") for hours worked over 40 in a workweek. Comp time is time off with pay in lieu of overtime pay. An employer and employees must agree that the employer will provide comp time. The agreement may be through a collective bargaining agreement or, if there is no such agreement, between the employer and individual employees. Comp time is calculated at a rate that is at least one-and-a-half times the number of overtime hours worked. In general, state and local government employees may accrue up to 240 hours of comp time. Law enforcement, fire protection, emergency response personnel, and employees engaged in seasonal activities may accrue up to 480 hours of comp time. Instead of providing comp time, an employer may pay an employee for any unused comp time. An employee must be allowed to use comp time on the date requested, unless doing so would "unduly disrupt" the operations of the agency.[31] Section 7(o) does not apply to state and local government employees who are exempt from overtime.[32]

Break Time for Nursing Mothers

The Patient Protection and Affordable Care Act (PPACA, P.L. 111-148) added new Section 7(r) to the FLSA.[33] Section 7 of the FLSA requires employers to pay at least time-and-a-half to employees who work overtime. Section 13 of the FLSA provides several exemptions to the overtime requirements of Section 7. Thus, new Section 7(r) does not apply to employers or employees who are exempt from overtime. Section 7(r) requires covered employers to provide break time for nursing mothers. Break time must be provided for one year after the child's birth. Employers must provide space, other than a bathroom, that is shielded from view and free from intrusion from coworkers and the public. Only employees who are not exempt from the FLSA's overtime pay requirements are entitled to break times to express milk. Employers with fewer than 50 employees are not subject to the requirement if compliance would impose an undue hardship on the employer. Employers are not required to compensate nursing mothers for breaks taken for the purpose of expressing milk.

EXEMPTIONS FROM THE MINIMUM WAGE OR OVERTIME STANDARDS OF THE FLSA

Most wage and salary workers are covered by the FLSA. However, under Section 13 of the act certain employers and employees are exempt from coverage. They may be exempt from either the minimum wage or overtime standards of the act, or both. This section considers some, but not all, of the current exemptions in Section 13. The focus is on those exemptions that have been the subject of recent legislation, hearings, or oversight.

Executive, Administrative, and Professional Employees

When the Fair Labor Standards Act (P.L. 75-718) was enacted in 1938, Section 13(a)(1) provided an exemption, from both the minimum wage and overtime requirements of the act, for bona fide executive, administrative, and professional employees (the EAP exemption).[34] The act did not define the terms executive, administrative, or professional employee. Instead, the law stated that the terms would be defined in regulations issued by the Secretary of Labor.[35]

Under current regulations, to qualify for the EAP exemption, employees must meet certain duties tests and be paid a salary of at least $455 per week.[36] Job titles do not determine whether an employee is exempt.

To qualify for the exemption for executive employees, all of the following job duties tests must be met:

- The employee's primary duty "is management of the enterprise in which the employee is employed or of a customarily recognized department or subdivision thereof";
- The employee "customarily and regularly directs the work of two or more other employees"; and
- The employee "has the authority to hire or fire other employees or whose suggestions and recommendations as to the hiring, firing, advancement, promotion or any other change of status of other employees are given particular weight."[37]

To qualify for the exemption for administrative employees, both of the following job duties tests must be met:

- The employee's primary duty "is the performance of office or nonmanual work directly related to the management or general business operations of the employer or the employer's customers;" and

- The employee's primary duty "includes the exercise of discretion and independent judgment with respect to matters of significance."[38]

To qualify for the exemption for professional employees, the following job duties test must be met:

- The employee's primary duty is the performance of work: "Requiring knowledge of an advanced type in a field of science or learning customarily acquired by a prolonged course of specialized intellectual instruction;" or "Requiring invention, imagination, originality or talent in a recognized field of artistic or creative endeavor."[39]

Periodically, DOL has modified the regulations that implement the EAP exemption. The regulations were last changed in 2004. The current minimum weekly salary of $455 is an issue in implementing the exemption. Between changes in the threshold, weekly salaries may rise because of inflation or increases in labor productivity.

Thus, unless the threshold is raised (either legislatively or administratively), over time more employees become exempt from overtime pay. On the other hand, a higher threshold may make it more difficult for employers to administer overtime (i.e., because employers would have to keep track of hours worked for more employees).

The job duties tests are a second issue in implementing the EAP exemption. For an employee to be exempt, the employee's job duties must meet the requirements for exemption. The tests are complex and can result in workers being misclassified (e.g., they may be classified as exempt when they should be nonexempt).

For employers, a higher salary threshold may make it easier to administer the job duties tests for exemption—because fewer employees would meet the minimum salary test.

Outside Salespersons

Outside salespersons are also exempt under Section 13(a)(1) of the FLSA. Unlike executive, administrative, and professional employees, however, the $455 salary test does not apply to outside salespersons.

To qualify for the exemption for outside sales employees, an employee must meet both of the following job duties tests:

- The employee's primary duty must be making sales (as defined in the FLSA), or obtaining orders or contracts for services or for the use of facilities for which a consideration will be paid by the client or customer;[40] and
- The employee must be customarily and regularly engaged away from the employer's place or places of business.[41]

An outside salesperson is someone who makes sales at the customer's home or place of business. The person may work hours that are convenient for the customer. Also, the hours worked by outside salespersons may be difficult for employers to monitor.

One issue with the exemption for outside salespersons is whether a sale involves the actual transfer of ownership of a company's goods or services. In a June 2012 decision by the U.S. Supreme Court, the court ruled that pharmaceutical sales representatives (also called "detailers") who encourage doctors to prescribe the use of a company's prescription drugs are outside salespersons, even though the drugs can only be sold with a doctor's prescription.[42]

Currently, regulations state that "Outside sales does not include sales made by mail, telephone or the Internet unless such contact is used merely as an adjunct to personal calls."[43] Some policymakers maintain that inside salespersons, whose primary duty is to make sales, should also be exempt.

Employees in Computer-Related Occupations

In 1990, Congress directed the Secretary of Labor to issue regulations that would exempt from overtime and the minimum wage certain employees in computer-related occupations.[44] Before 1990, computer employees could be exempt from FLSA coverage if they met the requirements of the EAP exemption. Regulations in effect in 1990 stated that the exemption for learned professionals applied to employees who have acquired "knowledge of an advanced type in a field of science or learning customarily acquired by a prolonged course of specialized intellectual instruction and study." The regulations said that knowledge of an "advanced type" was knowledge that generally could not be attained with only a high school degree. Rather, learned professionals typically held an "academic degree." The 1990 regulations went on to say that

> The question arises whether computer programmers and systems analysts in the data processing field are included in the learned professions. At the present time there is too great a variation in standards and academic requirements to conclude that employees employed in such occupations are a part of a true profession recognized as such by the academic community with universally accepted standards for employment in the field.[45]

In 1990, Congress enacted legislation that directed the Secretary of Labor to issue regulations that would allow "computer systems analysts, computer programmers, software engineers, and other similarly skilled professional workers" to qualify as exempt executive, administrative, or professional employees under Section 13(a)(1) of the FLSA. The 1990 legislation also directed the Secretary of Labor to apply the EAP exemption to employees in computer-related occupations if they were paid on an hourly wage that was at least six-and-a-half times the basic federal minimum wage.

In 1992, the U.S. Department of Labor (DOL) published final regulations that implemented the 1990 legislation. The regulations treated computer employees as professional employees under the EAP exemption. The regulations stated that the exemption applied to "highly skilled" computer employees. To be exempt as a professional employee, the 1992 regulations said that a computer employee's primary duty must consist of one or more of the following job duties:

> (1) The application of systems analysis techniques and procedures, including consulting with users, to determine hardware, software, or system functional specifications;
> (2) The design, development, documentation, analysis, creation, testing, or modification of computer systems or programs, including prototypes, based on and related to user or system design specifications;
> (3) The design, documentation, testing, creation or modification of computer programs related to machine operating systems; or
> (4) a combination of the aforementioned duties, the performance of which requires the same level of skills.

Finally, the 1992 regulations stated that "While such employees commonly have a bachelor's or higher degree, no particular academic degree is required for this exemption."[46]

When the final regulations implementing the 1990 legislation went into effect, the basic federal minimum wage was $4.25 an hour. Thus, computer employees who were paid by the hour were exempt if they met the new job duties test and were paid at least $27.63 an hour (i.e., 61/2 times $4.25).

In 1996, Congress added Section 13(a)(17) to the FLSA. Section 13(a)(17) applies specifically to employees in computer-related occupations. Under Section 13(a)(17), the minimum hourly wage for computer professionals was fixed at $27.63 an hour. The exemption includes in statute much of the language from the 1992 regulations that defined the primary duties of exempt computer professionals.

In 2004, DOL issued new regulations that revised the salary and duties tests for the EAP exemption. The regulations also simplified the duties tests for computer professionals to reflect the 1996 amendments to the FLSA. Under the 2004 regulations, computer professionals are exempt from the minimum wage and overtime standards of the FLSA if they meet the job duties test provided in regulations and, if they are paid an hourly wage, are paid at least $27.63 an hour or, if they are paid a salary, are paid at least $455 a week.[47] The same duties tests apply to both salaried and hourly computer employees.[48]

Skilled computer workers are not necessarily exempt from the minimum wage or overtime requirements of the FLSA. Employees engaged in the manufacture or repair of computer hardware are not exempt. Employees whose work is highly dependent on the use of computers and computer software programs (e.g., engineers, drafters and others skilled in computer-aided design software), but who are not primarily engaged in computer systems analysis and programming, are not exempt computer professionals.[49]

Domestic Service Employees

When the FLSA was enacted in 1938, it did not cover domestic service employees. The Fair Labor Standards Amendments of 1974 (P.L. 93-259) extended minimum wage and overtime coverage to include domestic service workers who are employed in private households.[50] Domestic service workers include housekeepers, cooks, full-time babysitters, and others.[51]

In addition to extending minimum wage and overtime coverage to domestic service employees, the 1974 amendments added two exemptions that affect two types of domestic service workers: domestic service workers who provide companionship services and live-in domestic service workers. Under Section 13(a)(15) of the FLSA, domestic service workers who provide companionship services in private homes are exempt from both the minimum wage and overtime standards of the act. Section 13(b)(21) of the act exempts from overtime, but not the minimum wage, domestic service workers who provide live-in domestic services.

On December 27, 2011, DOL issued a Notice of Proposed Rulemaking (NPRM) that would change the definition of companionship services.[52] Under current regulations:

- Companionship services are defined as "those services which provide fellowship, care, and protection for a person who, because of advanced age or physical or mental infirmity, cannot care for his or her own needs."
- Companionship services may include household work related to the care of the aged or infirmed individual, such as preparing meals, bed making, or washing clothes. General household work (such as housecleaning) may also be included in companionship services. However, general household work must be "incidental" to providing companionship services. Current regulations define incidental as 20% or less of the total hours worked.
- Companionship services do not include services performed by trained personnel, such as registered or practical nurses.[53]

The NPRM would narrow the exemption for companionship services. Under the proposed rule:

- The definition of companionship services would be limited to fellowship and protection (eliminating the reference to "care"). Fellowship and protection may include activities such as conversation, reading, watching television, going for walks, or visiting with friends of the person being cared for. A companion may also help the person use a wheelchair or walker and help the person move from one area of the home to another.
- Companions could spend up to 20% of total hours worked on incidental "intimate personal care" services. These services must be performed in conjunction with providing companionship services and may include occasional feeding, dressing, bathing, or grooming. A companion may occasionally drive the person to run errands or to appointments or social events. Incidental intimate personal care services would not include household work that benefits other

members of the household, such as housekeeping, making meals, or doing laundry.

- Companionship services would not include medical care provided by persons with specialized training.[54]

The proposed rule would also extend minimum wage and overtime coverage to companions employed by a third party employer, and extend overtime coverage to live-in domestic workers employed by a third party. The exemption for companions would continue to apply to companions employed directly by an individual or family (provided the companions meet the new definition of companionship services). Live-in domestic workers employed directly by individuals or families would still be exempt from overtime.[55]

DOL's target date for issuing a final rule is April 2013.[56]

CHILD LABOR

The FLSA sets minimum age requirements for youth employed outside of school hours in agricultural and nonagricultural occupations. In nonagricultural occupations, the act sets a general minimum age for employment of 16. In agricultural occupations, the general minimum age to work is 14.[57] The FLSA includes a number of exceptions to the general minimum age requirements of the act. Under a parental exemption, a child of any age may be employed by his or her parent (or person standing in the place of a parent) in any occupation in a business, including a farm, owned or operated by the parent. But, youth under 18 cannot be employed in mining or manufacturing, including in a business owned or operated by a parent.[58]

Youth under a certain age cannot work in occupations determined by the Secretary of Labor to be hazardous to minors. The minimum age to work in hazardous occupations in nonagricultural occupations is 18. In agricultural occupations, the minimum age is 16.

The FLSA also provides exemptions from the limits on employment in hazardous occupations. In agriculture, youth between the ages of 14 and 15 may work in certain hazardous occupations if they are student learners.[59] Minors ages 14 and 15 can operate tractors or other machinery if they hold a certificate of training from a 4-H or vocational agriculture training program. The restrictions on employment in hazardous occupations in agriculture do not apply to youth employed on farms owned or operated by a parent.

Youth ages 12 and 13 can work in agriculture with the written consent of their parents on a farm where a parent (or person standing in the place of a parent) is also employed.

Youth who are covered by the FLSA and are not exempt must be paid at least the applicable federal or state minimum wage. However, employees in agriculture are exempt from the overtime requirements of the FLSA.[60]

On September 2, 2011, DOL issued a proposed rule to change the regulations that implement the child labor provisions in agriculture. In the proposed rule, DOL said that "None of the revisions proposed in this NPRM in any way change or diminish the statutory child labor parental exemption in agricultural employment" in the FLSA.[61] Nevertheless, in response to concerns about the potential effects of the proposed rule on the parental exemption, DOL announced, on February 1, 2012, that it was going to reconsider the part of the rule dealing with the interpretation of the parental exemption. DOL said that instead of applying the parental exemption to farms that are "wholly" owned by the parent (or person standing in place of a parent), it would apply the parental exemption to farms that are "substantially" owned by the parent. Thus, the parental exemption would apply to farms where the parent is a part owner of the farm, a partner in a partnership, or an officer of a corporation that owns the farm if the parent holds a substantial ownership interest in the partnership or corporation.[62]

On April 26, 2012, DOL announced that it was withdrawing the proposed rule. DOL stated that "The decision to withdraw this rule—including provisions to define the 'parental exemption'— was made in response to thousands of comments expressing concerns about the effect of the proposed rules on small family-owned farms." DOL also stated that the regulation will not be pursued for the duration of the Obama Administration.[63]

APPENDIX. MAJOR AMENDMENTS TO THE FLSA, FEDERAL MINIMUM WAGE RATES, AND LIST OF ACRONYMS

This appendix briefly describes major amendments to the Fair Labor Standards Act (FLSA). *Table A-1* shows the history of legislated changes in the basic federal minimum wage. *Table A-2* shows the minimum wage rates in the states and other jurisdictions as of January 1, 2012. *Table A-3* provides a list of acronyms used in the report.

Major Amendments to the FLSA

The FLSA has been amended several times since 1938.[64] The amendments generally expanded coverage of the act, created subminimum wage rates, and increased the basic minimum wage.

1947 Amendments

In 1947, Congress passed the Portal-to-Portal Act. The act addressed issues arising out of several court cases. First, Congress addressed the practical definition of hours worked, for which an employee must be paid. Congress excluded from hours worked time spent traveling to and from work. Congress also stated that some "preliminary" and "postliminary" activities performed before or after the workday are not hours worked.[65] However, workers could be compensated for such activities if the worker and employer agreed to such employment terms or if compensation for the activities was customary in the place of employment.[66] The 1947 amendments also allow parties to settle a worker's minimum wage or overtime claim if "there exists a bona fide dispute as to the amount payable."[67] However, parties cannot agree to a settlement that would result in a wage less than the minimum wage or payment of less than timeand-a-half for overtime.[68]

Additionally, in the 1947 amendments Congress prohibited class action suits under the statute, unless the Secretary of Labor filed the suit as the representative of workers. It also limited the availability of compensation recovered in a class action suit only to those employees who affirmatively agreed to be a part of the suit.[69] Finally, the amendments set a two-year statute of limitation (time limit) in which a worker could file a claim.[70]

1961 and 1966 Amendments

In 1961, Congress amended FLSA exemptions such that employers of retail workers in enterprises with annual sales in excess of $1 million were required to pay minimum wage and overtime rates.[71]

In 1966, Congress expanded coverage of the FLSA to include workers employed in any enterprise with annual sales of at least $250,000 and employees of all businesses engaged in construction, repair, laundering, and cleaning services. Additionally, for the first time, FLSA coverage was extended to employees of hospitals, elementary and secondary schools, and institutions of higher education.[72] The 1966 amendments also added a "tip credit," which allowed employers to include a portion of an employee's tips as part of the minimum wage.[73] Finally, the 1966 amendments restricted the employment of youth under the age of 16 in agriculture in occupations found by the Secretary of Labor to be particularly hazardous, except when the employee is employed by a parent on a farm owned or operated by the parent.[74]

1974 Amendments

The 1974 FLSA amendments extended coverage to most federal, state, and local government employees. However, fire protection and law enforcement employees (including security personnel in correctional institutions) of public agencies were given special treatment, such as a complete exemption from overtime for agencies that employ fewer than five employees in fire protection or law enforcement and a partial exemption from overtime for fire protection and law enforcement employees who work from 7 to 28 consecutive days.[75]

1985 Amendments

In 1985, to ease the financial burden on state and local governments of paying overtime to significant numbers of employees, Congress amended the FLSA to allow public employers to offer their workers compensatory time off from work in lieu of overtime pay.[76]

1989 Amendments

In 1989, FLSA coverage was extended to enterprises with annual sales of at least $500,000. The amendments also repealed the retail exemption, under which employees of almost all small retail enterprises were exempt from the minimum wage and overtime rates.

The 1996 Small Business Job Protection Act

In 1996, Congress exempted certain computer professionals from minimum wage and overtime regulations.[77] The 1996 amendments also brought within the FLSA's minimum wage coverage all government employees employed as of April 1, 1996.

The 2007 Increases in the Basic Minimum Wage

On May 25, 2007, President George W. Bush signed into law a supplemental appropriations bill titled the "U.S. Troop Readiness, Veterans' Care, Katrina Recovery, and Iraq Accountability Appropriations Act, 2007" (P.L. 110-28). Title VIII of the act, "Fair Minimum Wage and Tax Relief," increased the basic federal minimum wage from $5.15 to $5.85 an hour effective July 2007, from $5.85 to $6.55 an hour effective July 2008, and from $6.55 to $7.25 an hour effective July 2009.

The Equal Pay Act

The Equal Pay Act (EPA), although commonly referred to on its own, was an amendment to the FLSA. The EPA was enacted in 1963 and prohibits gender-based pay discrimination.[78]

Break Time for Nursing Mothers

The 2010 Patient Protection and Affordable Care Act (PPACA) amended the FLSA to require covered employers to provide reasonable break time to nonexempt employees to express breast milk for a nursing child.

Table A-1. Federal Minimum Wage Laws

Public Law and Date Enacted	Wage Rate	Effective Date of Wage Rate
P.L. 75-718, enacted June 25, 1938	$0.25	October 1938
	0.30	October 1939
	0.40	October 1945
P.L. 81-393, enacted October 26, 1949	0.75	January 1950
P.L. 84-381, enacted August 12, 1955	1.00	March 1956
P.L. 87-30, enacted May 5, 1961	1.15	September 1961
	1.25	September 1963
P.L. 89-601, enacted September 23, 1966	1.40	February 1967
	1.60	February 1968
P.L. 93-259, enacted April 8, 1974	2.00	May 1974
	2.10	January 1975
	2.30	January 1976
P.L. 95-151, enacted November 1, 1977	2.65	January 1978
	2.90	January 1979
	3.10	January 1980
	3.35	January 1981
P.L. 101-157, enacted November 17, 1989	3.80	April 1990
	4.25	April 1991
P.L. 104-188, enacted August 20, 1996	4.75	October 1996
	5.15	September 1997
P.L. 110-28, enacted May 25, 2007	5.85	July 2007
	6.55	July 2008
	7.25	July 2009

Source: CRS Report RL33791, Possible Indexation of the Federal Minimum Wage: Evolution of Legislative Activity, by William G. Whittaker.

Table A-2. Minimum Wage Rates in the States and Other Jurisdictions, as of January 1, 2013

Jurisdictions (20) With Minimum Wage Rates Higher Than the Federal Minimum Wage		
Alaska ($7.75)	Illinois ($8.25)	New Mexico ($7.50)
Arizona ($7.80)	Maine ($7.50)	Ohio ($7.85)
California ($8.00)	Massachusetts ($8.00)	Oregon ($8.95)
Colorado ($7.78)	Michigan ($7.40)	Rhode Island ($7.75)
Connecticut ($8.25)	Missouri ($7.35)	Vermont ($8.60)
District of Columbia ($8.25)	Montana ($7.80)	Washington ($9.19)
Florida ($7.79)	Nevada ($8.25)	
Jurisdictions (24) With Minimum Wage Rates the Same as the Federal Minimum Wage ($7.25)		
Delaware	Maryland	Pennsylvania
Guam	Nebraska	South Dakota
Hawaii	New Hampshire	Texas
Idaho	New Jersey	Utah
Indiana	New York	U.S. Virgin Islands
Iowa	North Carolina	Virginia
Kansas	North Dakota	West Virginia
Kentucky	Oklahoma	Wisconsin
Jurisdictions (7) With Minimum Wage Rates Less Than the Federal Minimum Wage[a]		
American Samoa ($4.18-$5.59)[b]	Georgia ($5.15)	Puerto Rico ($4.10)
Arkansas ($6.25)	Minnesota ($6.15)	Wyoming ($5.15)
Commonwealth of the Northern Mariana Islands (CNMI) ($5.55)[b]		
Jurisdictions (5) With No State Minimum Wage Requirement[a]		
Alabama	Mississippi	Tennessee
Louisiana	South Carolina	

Source: U.S. Department of Labor, Wage and Hour Division, Changes in Basic Minimum Wages in Nonfarm Employment Under State Law: Selected Years 1968 To 2013, http://www.dol.gov/whd/state stateMinWageHis.htm#.UORh87 RHDAk. U.S. Department of Labor, Wage and Hour Division, Employee Rights Under the Fair Labor Standards Act, http://www.dol.gov/whd/regs/ compliance/posters/cnmi.pdf.

Notes: Coverage patterns vary from one jurisdiction to another. The table shows the highest wage applicable under current law.

[a] In states with a minimum wage that is lower than the federal minimum wage or with no minimum wage, state law applies to workers who are not covered by the FLSA.

[b] On September 30, 2012, the minimum wage in CNMI increased by $0.50 an hour to $5.55. In American Samoa, the next wage increases are scheduled for September 30, 2015. The rates will then rise every three years until they reach the federal minimum wage.

Table A-3. List of Acronyms

Acronym	Description
BLS	Bureau of Labor Statistics of the U.S. Department of Labor
CNMI	Commonwealth of the Northern Mariana Islands
CPI-U	Consumer Price Index for All Urban Consumers
DOL	U.S. Department of Labor
EAP	Executive, administrative, and professional employees
EPA	Equal Pay Act
FLSA	Fair Labor Standards Act
NIRA	National Industrial Recovery Act
NPRM	Notice of Proposed Rule Making
PPACA	Patient Protection and Affordable Care Act
SIC	Special Industrial Committees
SMW	Special minimum wage rates for persons with disabilities
SWEP	School Work Experience Program
WHD	Wage and Hour Division of the U.S. Department of Labor

End Notes

[1] Stephanie Fitzgerald, The New Deal: Rebuilding America (Minneapolis, MN: Compass Point Books, 2007), p. 77.

[2] This section of the report was written by Alexandra Hegji.

[3] Table A-3 in the Appendix provides a list of acronyms used in the report.

[4] U.S. Congress, House of Representatives Committee on Labor, Fair Labor Standards Act, Conference Report to Accompany S. 2475, 75th Cong., 3rd sess., June 11, 1938, Report No. 2738, p. 28.

[5] U.S. Congress, Senate Committee on Education and Labor, Fair Labor Standards Act, Report to Accompany S. 2475, 75th Cong., 1st sess., July 6, 1937, Report No. 884, p. 1.

[6] Fair Labor Standards Act of 1938, ch. 676, §§6, 7, and 12, 52 Stat. 1060, at 1062-64, 1067.

[7] Ibid.

[8] Although Congress articulated both social and economic reasons for regulating child labor, some commentators noted that President Roosevelt believed the addition of child labor provisions in the FLSA would make wage and hour provisions more palatable to Congress, thereby making FLSA enactment easier. Ibid.

[9] Fair Labor Standards Act of 1938, ch. 676, §§6, 7, 12, 52 Stat. 1060.

[10] Ibid., at 1067-1068.

[11] The size of an enterprise is measured by its "annual sales or business done." Annual sales or business done includes all business activities that can be measured in dollars. Thus, retailers are covered by the FLSA if their annual sales are at least $500,000. Owners of rental properties are covered if they collect at least $500,000 annually in rent. 29 C.F.R. §§779.258-779.259.

[12] U.S. Department of Labor, Wages and Hours Worked: Minimum Wage and Overtime Pay, available at http://www.dol.gov/compliance/guide/minwage.htm#who. 29 U.S.C. §203(s)(1).

[13] U.S. Department of Labor, Coverage Under the Fair Labor Standards Act, available at http://www.dol.gov/whd/ regs/compliance/whdfs14.pdf. (Hereafter cited as DOL, Coverage Under the Fair Labor Standards Act.)

[14] 29 U.S.C. §203(e).

[15] 29 U.S.C. §203(c).

[16] Other federal laws or regulations establish minimum wage requirements for workers. These rates are generally higher, but cannot be lower, than the applicable federal or state minimum wage. The Davis-Bacon Act requires employers to pay employees at least the locally prevailing wage and fringe benefits on construction contracts of more than $2,000 to which the federal government is a party. The Service Contract Act requires employers to pay workers at least the locally prevailing wage and fringe benefits on service contracts of more than $2,500 with the federal government. Unlike minimum wage rates under the FLSA, prevailing wages under the Davis-Bacon Act and Service Contract Act are not legislated by Congress. Rather, prevailing wages under the two acts are based on wage surveys conducted by or for the U.S. Department of Labor. As required by the Immigration and Nationality Act (INA) or regulations, minimum wage requirements also apply to foreign workers entering the United States under certain permanent employment-based visas and temporary nonimmigrant visas (e.g., the H-1B visa for temporary professional workers, the H-2A visa for temporary agricultural workers, and the H-2B visa for temporary nonagricultural workers). The minimum wage requirements for these workers are generally based on wage surveys, collective bargaining agreements, or prevailing wages under the Davis-Bacon Act or Service Contract Act.

[17] See Table A-1 in the Appendix for a history of federal laws that increased the basic minimum wage.

[18] See Table A-2 in the Appendix for a list of state minimum wage rates.

[19] U.S. Department of Labor, Bureau of Labor Statistics, Characteristics of Minimum Wage Workers: 2011, March 2, 2012, http://www.bls.gov/cps/minwage2011.pdf.

[20] 29 U.S.C. §203(m). In 1966, when the tip credit was added to the FLSA, an employer could claim up to 50% of the minimum wage as a tip credit. In 1996, the minimum cash wage for tipped employees was set at $2.13 an hour, which was 50% of the, then, minimum wage of $4.25 an hour.

[21] The five states that do not have minimum wage laws are Alabama, Louisiana, Mississippi, South Carolina, and Tennessee. In Georgia, tipped employees are exempt from the state minimum wage law. Puerto Rico allows a lower minimum wage for tipped workers than for nontipped workers.

[22] For a legislative history of Section 14(c), see out-of-print CRS Report RL30674, Treatment of Workers with Disabilities Under Section 14(c) of the Fair Labor Standards Act, by William G. Whittaker (available to congressional clients upon request).

[23] The certificates also allow the payment of wages that are less than the prevailing wages on contracts subject to the Service Contract Act (SCA).

[24] 29 C.F.R. §525.

[25] 29 U.S.C. §206(g).

[26] 29 C.F.R. §§520.201(c), 520.501(a), and 520.506(a).

[27] For more information on minimum wages in the territories, see CRS Report RL30235, Minimum Wage in the Territories and Possessions of the United States: Application of the Fair Labor Standards Act, by William G. Whittaker.

[28] The full name of P.L. 110-28 is the U.S. Troop Readiness, Veterans' Care, Katrina Recovery, and Iraq Accountability Appropriations Act, 2007.

[29] The title of the 2010 legislation is To Clarify the Availability of Existing Funds for Political Status Education in the Territory of Guam, and for Other Purposes (P.L. 111-244).

[30] Some states have overtime laws that are more protective of employees than the FLSA; for example, overtime pay may be required if an employee works more than 8 or 12 hours in a day. See U.S. Department of Labor, Wage and Hour Division, Wage and Hour Division (WHD) Minimum Wage Laws in the States, January 1, 2012, http://www.dol.gov/whd/minwage/america.htm.

[31] 29 C.F.R. §§553.20-553.28.

[32] Federal employees can receive comp time under the Federal Employees Flexible and Compressed Work Schedules Act of 1982 (P.L. 97-221). Comp time may be used by both exempt and nonexempt employees. U.S. Office of Personnel Management, Compensatory Time Off, http://www.opm.gov/OCA/pay/html/comp.htm.

[33] Section 7(r) of the FLSA was added by Section 4207, "Reasonable Break Time for Nursing Mothers," of PPACA.

[34] For more information on the exemption for executive, administrative, and professional employees, see CRS Report RL32088, The Fair Labor Standards Act: A Historical Sketch of the Overtime Pay Requirements of Section 13(a)(1), by William G. Whittaker.

[35] Originally, the FLSA stated that regulations implementing the EAP exemption would be issued by the administrator of the newly created Wage and Hour Division (WHD) of DOL. The Fair Labor Standards Amendments of 1961 (P.L. 87-30) changed the authority to issue regulations from the administrator of the WHD to the Secretary of Labor.

[36] An employee whose total annual compensation is at least $100,000 is exempt if he or she "customarily and regularly" performs at least one of the job duties tests for executive, administrative, or professional employees. 29 C.F.R. §541.601. Before 2004, under Section 13(a)(1), executive, administrative, or professional employees were exempt if they met either a long or a short test. Under both tests, to be exempt, an employee had to meet both a salary test and a job duties test. U.S. Department of Labor, Wage and Hour Division, "Defining and Delimiting the Terms 'Any Employee Employed in a Bona Fide Executive, Administrative, Professional, or Local Retailing Capacity, or in the Capacity of Outside Salesman,'" Federal Register, vol. 5, October 15, 1940, pp. 4077-4078.

[37] 29 C.F.R. §541.100.

[38] 29 C.F.R. §541.200.

[39] 29 C.F.R. §541.300.

[40] Obtaining orders for "the use of facilities" includes selling advertising time on radio, television, or in newspapers, and soliciting freight for railroads or other transportation companies. U.S. Department of Labor, Wage and Hour Division, Exemption for Outside Sales Employees Under the Fair labor Standards Act (FLSA), http://www.dol.gov/whd/regs/compliance/fairpay/fs17f_outsidesales.pdf.

[41] 29 C.F.R. §541.500.

[42] Christopher v. SmithKline Beecham Corp., No. 11-204, pp. 4-5, 14-15 (U.S. Supreme Court 2012).

[43] 29 C.F.R. §541.502.

[44] For more on the exemption for employees in computer-related occupations, see CRS Report, CRS Report R42141, Computer-Related Occupations Under the Fair Labor Standards Act (FLSA), by Gerald Mayer.

[45] 29 C.F.R. §§541.302 (July 1, 1990, edition).

[46] U.S. Department of Labor, Wage and Hour Division, "Fair Labor Standards Act: Computer-Related Occupations; Exemption from Minimum Wage and Overtime Compensation Requirements; Final Rule," Federal Register, vol. 57, October 9, 1992, p. 46744.

[47] The minimum weekly salary of $455 may be paid in periods longer than a week (e.g., $910 biweekly or $1,971.66 a month). 29 C.F.R. §541.600(b).

[48] 29 C.F.R. §541.400(b).

[49] 29 C.F.R. §541.401.

[50] The 1974 amendments added Sections 6(f) and 7(l) to the FLSA. Section 6(f) extended minimum wage coverage to domestic service employees. Section 6(f) states that Any employee (1) who in any workweek is employed in domestic service in a household shall be paid wages at a rate not less than the wage rate in effect under subsection (b) of this section unless such employee's compensation for such service would not because of section 209(a)(6) of the Social Security Act (42 U.S.C. 409(a)(6)) constitute wages for the purposes of title II of such Act (42 U.S.C. 401 et seq.), [i.e., the employee's pay must be wages for purposes of Social Security] or (2) who in any workweek (A) is employed in domestic service in one or more households, and (B) is so employed for more than 8 hours in the aggregate, shall be paid wages for such employment in such workweek at a rate not less than the wage rate in effect under subsection (b) of this section. [Note: Section 6(b) requires employers to pay employees at least the minimum wage rate required in Section 6(a) of the FLSA.] Section 7(l) extended overtime coverage to domestic service employees. Section 7(l) states that No employer shall employ any employee in domestic service in one or more households for a workweek longer than forty hours unless such employee receives compensation for such employment in accordance with subsection (a) of this section. [Note: Section 7(a) requires employers to pay covered employees at least one-and-a-half times their regular rate of pay for overtime.]

[51] DOL, Coverage Under the Fair Labor Standards Act.

[52] U.S. Department of Labor, Wage and Hour Division, "Application of the Fair Labor Standards Act to Domestic Service," Federal Register, vol. 76, December 27, 2011, pp. 81190-81244. (Hereafter cited as DOL, Application of the Fair Labor Standards Act to Domestic Service.) DOL twice extended the comment period on the proposed rule. Comments were due on or before March 21, 2012. U.S. Department of Labor, Wage and Hour Division, "Application of the Fair Labor Standards Act to Domestic Service," Federal Register, vol. 77, March 13, 2012, pp. 14688-14689.

[53] 29 C.F.R. §552.6. DOL, Application of the Fair Labor Standards Act to Domestic Service, p. 81195. A registered nurse may be exempt from the minimum wage and overtime standards of the FLSA as a professional employee under section 13(a)(1) of the act.

[54] DOL, Application of the Fair Labor Standards Act to Domestic Service, pp. 81193-81195, 81244.

[55] Ibid., pp. 81195-81196.

[56] Office of Information and Regulatory Affairs, Office of Management and Budget, Application of the Fair Labor Standards Act to Domestic Service, RIN1235-AA05, http://www.reginfo.gov/.

[57] For more information on child labor, see CRS Report RL31501, Child Labor in America: History, Policy, and Legislative Issues, by Gerald Mayer.

[58] Information on the age limits for youth employment are from U. S. Department of Labor, Wage and Hour Division, Child Labor Requirements in Agricultural Occupations Under the Fair Labor Standards Act, Child Labor Bulletin 102, available at http://www.dol.gov/whd/regs/compliance/childlabor102.pdf; and U. S. Department of Labor, Wage and Hour Division, Child Labor Provisions in Nonagricultural Occupations Under the Fair Labor Standards Act, Child Labor Bulletin 101, available at http://www.dol.gov/whd/regs/compliance/childlabor101.pdf.

[59] A student learner is someone who is enrolled in a vocational education program in agriculture under a written agreement that, among other things, ensures that the work of the student is incidental to the training.

[60] 29 U.S.C. 213(b)(12). Employees on small farms are exempt from both the minimum wage and overtime requirements of the FLSA. A farmer who did not employ more than 500 "man days" of labor in any calendar quarter in the preceding calendar year is exempt from the minimum wage and overtime requirements of the act. A "man day" is any day in which an employee performed agricultural work for at least one hour.

[61] U.S. Department of Labor, Wage and Hour Division, "Child Labor Regulations, Orders and Statements of Interpretation; Child Labor Violations—Civil Money Penalties," Federal Register, vol. 76, September 2, 2011, available at http://www.gpo.gov/fdsys/pkg/FR-2011-09-02/pdf/2011-21924.pdf, p. 54841.

[62] U.S. Department of Labor, Wage and Hour Division, U.S. Labor Department to Re-Propose 'Parental Exemption' of Child Labor in Agriculture Rule, February 1, 2012, http://www.dol.gov/opa/media/press/whd/WHD20120203.htm.

[63] U.S. Department of Labor, Wage and Hour Division, Labor Department Statement on Withdrawal of Proposed Rule Dealing With Children Who Work in Agricultural Vocations, http://www.dol.gov/opa/media/press/whd/ WHD20120826.htm.

[64] The review of major amendments to the FLSA was written by Alexandra Hegji.

[65] For instance, absent an employer-worker agreement or workplace custom, employers may not be required to pay workers minimum wage or overtime pay for the time workers spend changing clothes at the beginning and end of shifts while on work premises. See, for example, Genuth v. National Biscuit Co., 81 F. Supp. 213 (S.D.N.Y. 1948).

[66] 29 U.S.C. §252.

[67] 29 U.S.C. §253(a).

[68] Ibid.

[69] 29 U.S.C. §216.

[70] 29 U.S.C. §255.

[71] Fair Labor Standards Amendments of 1961, P.L. 87-30.

[72] 1966 U.S.C.C.A.N. §3003, 3008.

[73] 29 U.S.C. §203(m).

[74] U.S. House of Representatives, Fair Labor Standards Amendments of 1966, Conference Report to Accompany H.R. H.R. 13712, 89th Cong., 2nd sess., Report No. 2004, September 6, 1966, p. 18.

[75] Fair Labor Standards Amendments, 1974, P.L. 93-259.

[76] Fair Labor Standards Amendments of 1985, P.L. 99-150.

[77] 29 U.S.C. §213(a)(17).

[78] 29 U.S.C. §§206-209.

In: The Fair Labor Standards Act …
Editor: Julian A. Sotelo
ISBN: 978-1-62808-301-9

Chapter 2

COMPUTER-RELATED OCCUPATIONS UNDER THE FAIR LABOR STANDARDS ACT (FLSA)*

Gerald Mayer

SUMMARY

The Fair Labor Standards Act (FLSA) sets minimum standards for hourly wages, overtime pay, and child labor. The FLSA requires employers to pay covered employees at least $7.25 an hour and at least one-and-a-half times their regular hourly wage for hours worked over 40 hours a week at a given job. However, the FLSA includes a number of exemptions that exclude certain employees from the minimum wage and overtime standards of the act.

Section 13(a)(1) of the FLSA exempts from both the minimum wage and overtime pay standards of the act any person who is employed in a bona fide executive, administrative, or professional occupation (the EAP exemption). Before 1990, employees in computer-related occupations were exempt if they met the requirements of the EAP exemption.

In 1990, Congress directed the Secretary of Labor to issue regulations that would allow "computer systems analysts, computer programmers, software engineers, and other similarly skilled professional

---

* This is an edited, reformatted and augmented version of a Congressional Research Service publication, CRS Report for Congress R42141, from www.crs.gov, prepared for Members and Committees of Congress, dated February 24, 2012.

workers" to qualify as exempt executive, administrative, or professional employees under Section 13(a)(1) of the FLSA. The 1990 legislation also directed Congress to apply the EAP exemption to employees in computer-related occupations if they were paid on an hourly basis at a rate of at least six-and-a-half times the basic federal minimum wage. At the time, the federal minimum wage was $4.25 an hour. Thus, hourly computer employees were exempt if they met the job duties test and were paid at least $27.63 an hour. In 1992, the U.S. Department of Labor (DOL) published a final rule that implemented the 1990 legislation. The regulations treated computer employees as professional employees under the EAP exemption.

In 1996, Congress amended the FLSA to add a specific exemption for computer employees. The amendments fixed the minimum hourly wage for computer professionals at $27.63 an hour and included in statute much of the regulatory language from the 1992 regulations that defined the primary duties of computer professionals.

In 2004, DOL issued new regulations that revised the salary and duties tests for the EAP exemption. The regulations also simplified the duties test for computer professionals to reflect the 1996 amendments to the FLSA. Under the 2004 regulations, whether they are paid by the hour (at a minimum rate of $27.63) or the week (at a minimum rate of $455), computer professionals are exempt from the minimum wage and overtime standards of the FLSA if they meet the job duties test provided in regulations.

Employees in certain computer-related occupations are not exempt and must be paid at least the minimum wage and time-and-a-half for overtime. The exemption for workers in computer occupations does not include employees engaged in the manufacture or repair of computer hardware. Employees whose work is highly dependent on the use of computers but who are not engaged primarily in computer systems analysis, programming, or other similarly skilled computer occupations are not exempt. Depending on their job duties, Information Technology (IT) Support Specialists may not be exempt from the minimum wage and overtime standards of the FLSA.

In recent Congresses, legislation has been introduced that would expand the statutory exemption for computer employees to include workers whose job duties include network or database analysis and workers who manage or train employees who qualify for the exemption.

INTRODUCTION

The Fair Labor Standards Act (FLSA) sets minimum standards for hourly wages, overtime pay, and child labor.[1] The FLSA requires employers to pay covered employees at least $7.25 an hour. [2] The act also requires employers to pay covered workers at least one-and-ahalf times their regular hourly wage for hours worked over 40 hours a week at a given job.

The FLSA includes a number of exemptions that exclude certain employees from the minimum wage and overtime standards of the act. Exemptions apply to higher-paid professional and other employees, employees who may not work a fixed schedule from week to week, and employees whose work hours may be difficult for employers to monitor. In both 1990 and 1996, Congress amended the FLSA to exempt certain computer-related occupations from the minimum wage and overtime standards of the act.

Under current law, computer systems analysts, programmers, software engineers, and similarly skilled computer employees are exempt from both the minimum wage and overtime requirements of the FLSA. Computer professionals are exempt if they meet a job duties test and are paid a salary of at least $455 a week or a wage of at least $27.63 an hour.

Given recent interest in potential changes to the FLSA affecting workers in computer-related occupations, this report explains the exemption for computer employees and the regulations that implement the exemption. In addition, the report describes those computer occupations that are not exempt from either the minimum wage or overtime standards of the FLSA.

In recent Congresses, legislation has been introduced that would expand the statutory exemption for computer employees to include workers whose job duties include network or database analysis and workers who manage or train employees who qualify for the exemption. Thus, the final section of the report summarizes recent legislation to expand the exemption for employees in computer-related occupations.

Policy Objectives of a Minimum Wage and Time-and-a-Half for Overtime

Several reasons have been offered to justify a statutory minimum wage. One argument is that no worker should be paid less than a living wage. Another argument is that a fair wage should be paid to workers employed in jobs that require limited skills. A third argument for a minimum wage is that it can increase the purchasing power of low-wage workers and, therefore, raise aggregate demand for goods and services and reduce unemployment. In opposing a minimum wage, others argue that it diminishes the employment opportunities of less-skilled workers and does little to raise the incomes of low-income families—because many low-wage workers do not live in low-income families or because many low-income families do not have earners.[3]

Requiring employers to pay time-and-a-half for overtime has two policy objectives. First, timeand-a-half is intended to reduce involuntary unemployment. It is argued that paying more for overtime hours can shorten the workweek and increase overall employment. The second reason for overtime pay is to reduce overwork. During debate over the FLSA, proponents argued that some employees work overly long hours, which is harmful to individual health and public safety. Opponents of overtime pay argue that it does not increase employment and amounts to government interference in labor markets.[4]

THE FLSA EXEMPTION FOR PROFESSIONAL EMPLOYEES

When the Fair Labor Standards Act (P.L. 75-718) was enacted in 1938, Section 13(a)(1) provided an exemption, from both the minimum wage and overtime sections of the act, for bona fide executive, administrative, and professional employees (the EAP exemption). The act did not define the terms executive, administrative, or professional employee. Instead, the law stated that the terms would be defined in regulations issued by the administrator of the newly created Wage and Hour Division (WHD) of DOL.[5] Under regulations issued by the administrator, executive, administrative, and professional employees were exempt if they met both a salary test and a job duties test.[6]

Employees in computer occupations may be exempt from the minimum wage and overtime standards of the FLSA under the EAP exemption. In addition, in 1990 Congress amended the FLSA to exempt certain employees in computer-related occupations. Regulations that implemented the 1990 amendments treated computer employees as professional employees. Professional employees include the traditional professions of law and medicine, but they also include engineers, accountants, nurses, social workers, and others.[7]

During hearings and debate before the FLSA was passed in 1938, very little was said about the reasons for the exemption for professional employees.[8] The exemption had its roots in the National Industrial Relations

Act of 1933 (NIRA, P.L. 73-67).[9] In addition to funding public works projects, the NIRA allowed industries to establish "codes of fair competition."[10] Many of these codes excluded professional employees from any minimum wage and overtime pay requirements.[11]

Despite limited congressional discussion of the reasons for the professional exemption, two explanations are often given. The most common justification for the exemption is that, compared to less-skilled workers, professional employees are better able to bargain individually over wages, hours, and working conditions.[12] A second explanation is that professional employees may not work a fixed schedule. They may be called on to work evenings or weekends. In addition, if they travel it may be difficult for employers to monitor the total number of hours worked.[13]

THE 1990 AMENDMENTS TO THE FLSA

The remainder of this report describes amendments to the FLSA and regulations that affect employees in computer-related occupations. After a review of these amendments, the report summarizes legislative proposals in recent Congresses that would expand the exemption for computer employees.

With the development of computer technology and the growth of computer-related occupations, Congress amended the FLSA to exempt certain employees in computer-related occupations. In 1990, Congress directed the Secretary of Labor to include certain computer employees in the EAP exemption. The 1990 amendments (P.L. 101-583)[14] stated that the Secretary of Labor must issue regulations that would allow "computer systems analysts, computer programmers, software engineers, and other similarly skilled professional workers as defined in such regulations to qualify as exempt executive, administrative, or professional employees under Section 13(a)(1)" of the FLSA.[15]

P.L. 101-583 also directed Congress to apply the EAP exemption to employees in computer-related occupations if they were paid on an hourly basis at a rate of at least six-and-a-half times the basic federal minimum wage. At the time, the federal minimum wage was $4.25 an hour. Thus, hourly computer employees were exempt if they met the job duties test and were paid at least $27.63 an hour.[16]

Regulations in Effect Before the 1990 Amendments to the FLSA

Before the 1990 amendments to the FLSA, DOL regulations explained why certain employees in computer-related occupations were not exempt as "learned professionals." The regulations stated that learned professionals require "knowledge of an advanced type in a field of science or learning customarily acquired by a prolonged course of specialized intellectual instruction and study." The regulations said that an academic degree, as opposed to just a high school education, was the best evidence of professional training. The regulations added that the areas where the professional exemption may apply were expanding. As knowledge is developed, academic degrees are offered in new fields and employees who are trained in these fields may be exempt as learned professionals. The regulations said that computer programmers and systems analysts were not learned professionals because there were no universally accepted academic requirements for employment in these occupations.[17]

At the time of the 1990 amendments to the FLSA, the EAP exemption applied to employees who met either a "long" or a "short" test. Under both tests, an employee had to be paid a salary and not an hourly wage. Salaried workers had to be paid their full salary for any week in which they worked, regardless of the number of days or hours they worked.[18]

Under the long test, an exempt professional employee had to be paid between $170 and $249.99 a week. The employee's primary duty had to consist of work that required advanced knowledge usually gained through a prolonged course of specialized instruction, that involved the consistent exercise of discretion and judgment, and that was mainly intellectual in character.[19]

Under the short test, exempt professional employees were paid at least $250 a week. Their primary duty included work that required the consistent exercise of discretion and judgment.[20] (See the *Appendix* for the relevant parts of the long and short tests in effect before the 1990 amendments to the FLSA.[21])

Regulations that Implemented the 1990 Amendments to the FLSA

In 1992, DOL published a final rule that implemented the 1990 amendments to the FLSA.[22] The regulations treated computer employees as professional employees under the EAP exemption. The 1992 regulations stated that professional employees included highly skilled workers employed as computer systems analysts, computer programmers, and software engineers, or in other skilled computer occupations. Regulations added language to exempt hourly employees who were paid at least $27.63 an hour. The weekly salary test for computer professionals remained the same as under prior regulations: between $170 and $249.99 under the long test and at least $250 under the short test. Finally, the regulations added language that detailed the primary duties of computer professionals.

The 1992 regulations added language to existing Code of Federal Regulations (C.F.R.) Section 541.3 and added new language to renumbered Section 541.303. Specifically, new Section 541.3(a)(4) stated that professional occupations include

> Work that requires theoretical and practical application of highly-specialized knowledge in computer systems analysis, programming, and software engineering, and who is employed and engaged in these activities as a computer systems analyst, computer programmer, software engineer, or other similarly skilled worker in the computer software field, as provided in Section 541.303.

New language covering hourly employees was added to existing Section 541.3(e). Revised Section 541.3(e) stated:

> That the salary or fee requirements of this paragraph shall not apply to an employee engaged in computer-related work within the scope of paragraph (a)(4) of this section and who is compensated on an hourly basis at a rate in excess of 6 times the minimum wage provided by Section 6 of the Act.

Finally, the 1992 regulations included language that described the primary duties of computer professionals. The relevant parts of renumbered Section 541.303 were as follows:

Computer related occupations under P.L. 101-583.

> (a) Pursuant to P.L. 101-583, enacted November 15, 1990, Section 541.3(a)(4) provides that computer systems analysts, computer programmers, software engineers, or other similarly skilled workers in the computer software field are eligible for exemption as professionals under Section 13(a)(1) of the Act. Employees who qualify for this exemption are highly-skilled in computer systems analysis, programming,

or related work in software functions. Employees who perform these types of work have varied job titles. Included among the more common job titles are computer programmer, systems analyst, computer systems analyst, computer programmer analyst, applications programmer, applications systems analyst, applications systems analyst/programmer, software engineer, software specialist, systems engineer, and systems specialist. These job titles are illustrative only and the list is not intended to be all-inclusive. Further, because of the wide variety of job titles applied to computer systems analysis and programming work, job titles alone are not determinative of the applicability of this exemption.

(b) To be considered for exemption under Section 541.3(a)(4), an employee's primary duty must consist of one or more of the following:

a) The application of systems analysis techniques and procedures, including consulting with users, to determine hardware, software, or system functional specifications;
b) The design, development, documentation, analysis, creation, testing, or modification of computer systems or programs, including prototypes, based on and related to user or system design specifications;
c) The design, documentation, testing, creation or modification of computer programs related to machine operating systems; or
d) a combination of the aforementioned duties, the performance of which requires the same level of skills.

(c) The exemption provided by Section 541.3(a)(4) applies only to highly-skilled employees who have achieved a level of proficiency in the theoretical and practical application of a body of highly-specialized knowledge in computer systems analysis, programming, and software engineering, and does not include trainees or employees in entry level positions learning to become proficient in such areas or to employees in these computer-related occupations who have not attained a level of skill and expertise which allows them to work independently and generally without close supervision. The level of expertise and skill required to qualify for this exemption is generally attained through combinations of education and experience in the field. While such employees commonly have a bachelor's or higher degree, no particular academic degree is required for this exemption, nor are there any requirements for licensure or certification, as is required for the exemption for the learned professions.

The 1992 final rule summarized responses to the proposed regulations. Several individuals commented that the 1990 amendments would deprive them of overtime pay. These individuals said that they were employed as computer systems analysts, programmers, and engineers and that they were generally employed by service contractors and were paid by the hour. Others commented that the minimum hourly wage to qualify for exemption was too high; that is, it should be less than six-and-a-half times the minimum wage of $4.25.[23]

THE 1996 AMENDMENTS TO THE FLSA

In 1996, Congress amended the FSLA to add a specific statutory exemption for computer professionals. P.L. 104-188 added Section 13(a)(17) to the FLSA.[24] The 1996 amendments fixed the minimum hourly wage for computer professionals paid on an hourly basis at $27.63 an hour. The amendments also included in statute much of the regulatory language from the 1992 regulations that defined the primary duties of computer professionals.

Under Section 13(a)(17) of the FLSA, the following employees are exempt from the minimum wage and overtime standards of the act:

> (17) any employee who is a computer systems analyst, computer programmer, software engineer, or other similarly skilled worker, whose primary duty is—
>
> (A)the application of systems analysis techniques and procedures, including consulting with users, to determine hardware, software, or system functional specifications;
>
> (B) the design, development, documentation, analysis, creation, testing, or modification of computer systems or programs, including prototypes, based on and related to user or system design specifications;
>
> (C)the design, documentation, testing, creation, or modification of computer programs related to machine operating systems; or
>
> (D) a combination of duties described in subparagraphs (A), (B), or (C) the performance of which requires the same level of skills, and
>
> who, in the case of an employee who is compensated on an hourly basis, is compensated at a rate of not less than $27.63 an hour.

THE 2004 REGULATIONS FOR COMPUTER PROFESSIONALS

After the 1996 amendments to the FLSA, DOL did not revise the regulations for computer professionals until 2004. A rule issued in 2004 revised the regulations that implement the EAP exemption. Instead of long and short tests, under the 2004 regulations professional employees are exempt if they are paid at least $455 a week (up from $170 under the long test and $250 under the short test).[25] As provided in the 1996 amendments to the FLSA, computer professionals paid by the hour are exempt if they meet the duties test and their hourly wage is at least $27.63.

The 2004 regulations combined language that had been in C.F.R. Sections 541.3(a)(4) and 541.303.[26] The revised duties test removed the requirement that exempt computer employees must consistently exercise discretion and independent judgment.

The 2004 regulations state that computer systems analysts, computer programmers, software engineers, and other similarly skilled computer workers are exempt from the minimum wage and overtime standards of the FLSA if they meet the weekly or hourly test and their primary duty consists of[27]

1) The application of systems analysis techniques and procedures, including consulting with users, to determine hardware, software, or system functional specifications;
2) The design, development, documentation, analysis, creation, testing, or modification of computer systems or programs, including prototypes, based on and related to user or system design specifications;
3) The design, documentation, testing, or modification of computer programs related to machine operating systems, or
4) A combination of the aforementioned duties, the performance of which requires the same level of skills.[28]

Nonexempt Employees in Computer-Related Occupations

Regulations that implemented the 1990 amendments to the FLSA identified certain computer-related occupations that are not exempt from the minimum wage and overtime standards of the FLSA. The 2004 regulations clarified the job duties of nonexempt computer employees.

According to the 2004 regulations, employees in computer-related occupations are exempt from the minimum wage and overtime standards of the FLSA if they meet both the job duties test and are paid a salary of at least $455 a week or a wage of at least $27.63 an hour. Job titles do not determine if a computer employee is exempt.[29] Skilled computer workers are not necessarily exempt.

According to the 2004 regulations, the following computer employees are not exempt:

> The exemption for employees in computer occupations does not include employees engaged in the manufacture or repair of computer hardware and related equipment. Employees whose work is highly dependent upon, or facilitated by, the use of computers and computer software programs (e.g., engineers, drafters and others skilled in computer-aided design software), but who are not primarily engaged in computer systems analysis and programming or other similarly skilled computer-related occupations identified in §541.400(b), are also not exempt computer professionals.[30]

In 2006, the Wage and Hour Division (WHD) of DOL issued an opinion letter in which it concluded that Information Technology (IT) Support Specialists are not exempt from the minimum wage and overtime standards of the FLSA. As described by the employer who requested the opinion, the primary duty of IT Support Specialists is to install, configure, test, and troubleshoot computer applications, networks, and hardware. Based on the job duties provided by the employer, WHD concluded that IT Support Specialists are not exempt as computer professionals.[31]

LEGISLATION

The remainder of this report summarizes legislation, beginning with the 112th Congress, to amend Section 13(a)(17) of the FLSA. The section ends with legislation from the 106th Congress, when the House of Representatives passed legislation that would have amended Section 13(a)(17). The measure was not considered in the Senate.

112th Congress

In the 112th Congress, Senator Kay Hagan introduced S. 1747, the Computer Professionals Update Act. S. 1747 would amend Section 13(a)(17) of the FLSA to cover employees who work in a computer or IT occupation as an analyst, programmer, engineer, designer, developer, or other similarly skilled worker. Administrators would be included in computer- and IT-related occupations. The job duties test would be expanded to include employees whose primary duty includes the application of network or database analysis techniques. The duties test would include employees who direct the work, train, or lead teams of employees who meet the modified job duties test. As amended, Section 13(a)(17) would apply to employees in computer- and IT-related occupations who are paid on an hourly basis at a rate of at least $27.63 an hour and employees who are paid on a salary basis as provided in regulations (currently, $455 a week).

S. 1747 would amend 13(a)(17) of the FLSA to exempt

> (17) any employee working in a computer or information technology occupation (including, but not limited to, work related to computers, information systems, components, networks, software, hardware, databases, security, internet, intranet, or websites) as an analyst, programmer, engineer, designer, developer, administrator, or other similarly skilled worker, whose primary duty is—
>
> (A) the application of systems, network or database analysis techniques and procedures, including consulting with users, to determine or modify hardware, software, network, database, or system functional specifications;
> (B) the design, development, documentation, analysis, creation, testing, securing, configuration, integration, debugging, modification of computer or information technology, or enabling continuity of systems and applications;
> (C) directing the work of individuals performing duties described in subparagraph (A) or (B), including training such individuals or leading teams performing such duties; or
> (D) a combination of duties described in subparagraphs (A), (B), and (C), the performance of which requires the same level of skill;
>
> who is compensated at an hourly rate of not less than $27.63 an hour or who is paid on a salary basis at a salary level as set forth by the

Department of Labor in part 541 of title 29, Code of Federal Regulations. An employee described in this paragraph shall be considered an employee in a professional capacity pursuant to paragraph (1).

108th Congress

Senator Lindsey Graham introduced S. 495 ("a bill to amend the Fair Labor Standards Act of 1938 to clarify the exemption from the minimum wage and overtime compensation requirements of that Act for certain computer professionals"). A companion bill, H.R. 1996, was introduced in the House by Representative Joe Wilson.

S. 495 would have amended the FLSA to extend the exemption for employees in computer-related occupations to include network and database analysts, designers, and developers. The legislation would have modified the job duties test to include employees whose primary duty was the application of network or database analysis techniques and procedures. Computer employees would have been exempt if their primary duty was to configure, integrate, or secure or resolve problems for computer systems, networks, databases, or programs. Employees whose primary duty was to manage or train employees who met the modified job duties test would have been exempt.

S. 495/H.R. 1996 would have amended 13(a)(17) of the FLSA to exempt

> (17)(A) any employee who is a computer systems, network, or database analyst, designer, developer, programmer, software engineer, or other similarly skilled worker—
>
> (i) whose primary duty is—
>
> (I) the application of systems or network or database analysis techniques and procedures, including consulting with users, to determine hardware, software, systems, network, or database specifications (including functional specifications);
>
> (II) the design, configuration, development, integration, documentation, analysis, creation, testing, securing, or modification of, or problem resolution for, computer systems, networks, databases, or programs, including prototypes, based on and related to user, system, network, or database specifications, including design specifications and machine operating systems;
>
> (III) the management or training of employees performing duties described in subclause (I) or (II); or

(IV) a combination of duties described in subclauses (I), (II), or (III) the performance of which requires the same level of skills; and

(ii) who, in the case of an employee who is compensated on an hourly basis, is compensated at a rate of not less than $27.63 an hour.

(B) In this paragraph, the term 'network' includes the Internet and Intranet networks and the world wide web.

(C) For the purposes of this Act, an employee who meets the exemption provided by this paragraph shall be considered an employee in a professional capacity under paragraph (1).

107th Congress

Representative Robert Andrews introduced H.R. 1545 ("a bill to amend the Fair Labor Standards Act of 1938 to clarify the exemption from the minimum wage and overtime compensation requirements of that Act for certain computer professionals"). Similar language was included in H.R. 546, a bill introduced by Representative Jack Quinn. The latter bill was titled the Small Business Tax Fairness Act of 2001.

H.R. 1545/H.R. 546 would have amended the FLSA to extend the exemption for employees in computer-related occupations to include network and database analysts, designers, and developers. Both bills would have extended the exemption for employees in computer-related occupations to include network and database analysts, designers, and developers. The legislation would have modified the job duties test to include employees whose primary duty was the application of network or database analysis techniques and procedures.

Computer employees would have been exempt if their primary duty was to configure, integrate, or secure or resolve problems for computer systems, networks, databases, or programs. Employees would have been exempt if their primary duty was to manage or train employees who met the modified job duties test.

H.R. 1545 and Section 603 of H.R. 546 would have amended Section 13(a)(17) to exempt

(17) any employee who is a computer systems, network, or database analyst, designer, developer, programmer, software engineer, or other similarly skilled worker—

(A) whose primary duty is—

(I) the application of systems or network or database analysis techniques and procedures, including consulting with users, to determine hardware, software, systems, network, or database specifications (including functional specifications);

(II) the design, configuration, development, integration, documentation, analysis, creation, testing, securing, or modification of, or problem resolution for, computer systems, networks, databases, or programs, including prototypes, based on and related to user, system, network, or database specifications, including design specifications and machine operating systems;

(III) the management or training of employees performing duties described in clause (i) or (ii); or

(IV) a combination of duties described in clauses (i), (ii), or (iii) the performance of which requires the same level of skills; and

(B) who, in the case of an employee who is compensated on an hourly basis, is compensated at a rate of not less than $27.63 an hour.

For purposes of this paragraph, the term 'network' includes the Internet and intranet networks and the world wide web. An employee who meets the exemption provided by this paragraph shall be considered an employee in a professional capacity pursuant to paragraph (1).

106th Congress

In the 106th Congress, the House approved legislation that would have amended Section 13(a)(17) of the FLSA. The Senate did not consider the measure.

Representative Robert Andrews introduced H.R. 3038 ("a bill to amend the Fair Labor Standards Act of 1938 to clarify the exemption from the minimum wage and overtime compensation requirements of that Act for certain computer professionals").

Representative John Shimkus introduced H.R. 3846 ("a bill to amend the Fair Labor Standards Act of 1938 to increase the minimum wage, and for other purposes"). H.R. 3846 was passed by the House and appended to H.R. 3081, the Small Business Tax Fairness Act of 2000. H.R. 3081 was sponsored by Representative Rick Lazio. H.R. 3081 passed the House, but the Senate did not take up the bill.

H.R. 3846, as added to H.R. 3081 (as §603) would have amended Section 13(a)(17) to exempt

(17) any employee who is a computer systems, network, or database analyst, designer, developer, programmer, software engineer, or other similarly skilled worker—

(A) whose primary duty is—

(I) the application of systems or network or database analysis techniques and procedures, including consulting with users, to determine hardware, software, systems, network, or database specifications (including functional specifications);
(II) the design, configuration, development, integration, documentation, analysis, creation, testing, securing, or modification of, or problem resolution for, computer systems, networks, databases, or programs, including prototypes, based on and related to user, system, network, or database specifications, including design specifications and machine operating systems;
(III) the management or training of employees performing duties described in clause (i) or (ii); or
(IV) a combination of duties described in clauses (i), (ii), or (iii) the performance of which requires the same level of skills; and

(B) who, in the case of an employee who is compensated on an hourly basis, is compensated at a rate of not less than $27.63 an hour.

For purposes of paragraph (17), the term 'network' includes the Internet and intranet networks and the world wide web. An employee who meets the exemption provided by paragraph (17) shall be considered an employee in a professional capacity pursuant to paragraph (1).

APPENDIX. REGULATIONS FOR PROFESSIONAL EMPLOYEES IN EFFECT BEFORE THE 1990 AMENDMENTS TO THE FLSA

In 1990, Congress directed the Secretary of Labor to issue regulations that would exempt certain employees in computer-related occupations from the minimum wage and overtime standards of the FLSA. At the time, under

Section 13(a)(1), executive, administrative, or professional employees were exempt if they met either a long or a short test.

Long Test

Under the long test, an exempt professional employee was paid between $170 and $249.99 a week. Under the long test, a professional employee was an employee

(a) Whose primary duty consists of the performance of:

(I) Work requiring knowledge of an advance type in a field of science or learning customarily acquired by a prolonged course of specialized intellectual instruction and study, as distinguished from a general academic education and from an apprenticeship, and from training in the performance of routine mental, manual, or physical processes, or

(II) Work that is original and creative in character in a recognized field of artistic endeavor (as opposed to work which can be produced by a person endowed with general manual or intellectual ability and training), and the result of which depends primarily on the invention, imagination, or talent of the employee, or

(III) Teaching, tutoring, instructing, or lecturing in the activity of imparting knowledge and who is employed and engaged in this activity as a teacher in the school system or educational establishment or institution by which he is employed; and

(b) Whose work requires the consistent exercise of discretion and judgment in its performance; and

(c) Whose work is predominantly intellectual and varied in character (as opposed to routine mental, manual, mechanical, or physical work) and is of such character that the output produced or the result accomplished cannot be standardized in relation to a given period of time; and

(d) Who does not devote more than 20 percent of his hours worked in the workweek to activities which are not an essential part of and necessarily incident to the work described in paragraphs (a) through (c) of this section; and

(e) Who is compensated for services on a salary or fee basis at a rate of not less than $170 per week....

Short Test

Under the short test, an exempt professional employee was paid at least $250 a week. Under the short test, a professional employee was an employee whose occupation "includes work requiring the consistent exercise of discretion and judgment or of work requiring invention, imagination, or talent in a recognized field of artistic endeavor...."[32]

End Notes

[1] The FLSA, as amended, is located at 29 U.S.C. §§201-219.

[2] The FLSA has lower minimum wage rates for tipped employees; new hires under the age of 20; full-time students who work in retail or service establishments, agriculture, or institutions of higher education; high school students who are at least 16 and enrolled in a vocational education program; and handicapped persons. Several states have minimum wage rates that are higher than the basic federal minimum wage of $7.25. If a state minimum wage is higher than the federal wage, the higher state wage applies.

[3] See CRS Report RL30927, The Federal Minimum Wage: The Issue of Indexation, by Gerald Mayer.

[4] See CRS Report RL32349, The "White-Collar" Exemptions to Overtime Pay Under Current and Proposed Regulations: An Economic Analysis, by Gerald Mayer. For a discussion of whether time spent using personal data assistants (PDAs) and smart phones beyond the 40-hour workweek is eligible for overtime pay, see CRS Report R41993, The Fair Labor Standards Act, Overtime Compensation, and Personal Data Assistants, by Jon O. Shimabukuro.

[5] The Fair Labor Standards Amendments of 1961 (P.L. 87-30) changed the reference to the administrator of the WHD to the Secretary of the U.S. Department of Labor.

[6] U.S. Department of Labor, Wage and Hour Division, "Defining and Delimiting the Terms 'Any Employee Employed in a Bona Fide Executive, Administrative, Professional, or Local Retailing Capacity, or in the Capacity of Outside Salesman,'" Federal Register, vol. 5, October 15, 1940, pp. 4077-4078.

[7] Bureau of National Affairs, Wage and Hour Cases, January 1939-April 1946 (Washington, DC: Bureau of National Affairs, 1947), p. 441; Bureau of National Affairs, Wage and Hour Cases, April 1946-April 1961 (Washington, DC: Bureau of National Affairs, 1963), p. 447; Bureau of National Affairs, Wage and Hour Cases, 2005-2010 (Washington, DC: Bureau of National Affairs, 2011), p. 175.

[8] Eric Linder, Time and a Half's the American Way: A History of the Exclusion of White-Collar Workers from Overtime Regulation, 1868-2004 (Iowa City: Fănpihuà Press, 2004), pp. 385-386. (Hereafter cited as Linder, Time and a Half's the American Way.)

[9] John S. Forsythe, "Legislative History of the Fair Labor Standards Act," Law and Contemporary Problems, Summer 1939, p. 464. In 1935, the U.S. Supreme Court declared that the NIRA was unconstitutional.

[10] U.S. Congress, House of Representatives, Committee on Ways and Means, The National Recovery Administration: Message from the President of the United States, House Document 158, 75th Cong., 1st Sess., (Washington, DC: U.S. Government Print. Office, 1937), p. 1; Leverett S. Lyon et al., The National Recovery Administration: An Analysis and Appraisal (New York: Da Capo Press, 1972) (reprint of a 1935 edition published by the Brookings Institution), pp. 8-9.

[11] Linder, Time and a Half's the American Way, pp. 260-261.

[12] Peter D. DeChiara, "Rethinking The Managerial-Professional Exemption of The Fair Labor Standards Act," American University Law Review, vol. 53, 1993, p. 165.

[13] Ibid., p. 182.

[14] The title of P.L. 101-583 (S. 2930) is "a bill to eliminate 'substantial documentary evidence' requirement for minimum wage determination for American Samoa."

[15] U.S. Department of Labor, Wage and Hour Division, "Computer Employees Professional Exemption," Field Assistance Bulletin No. 2006-3, December 14, 2006, available at http://www.dol.gov/whd/FieldBulletins/ FieldAssistanceBulletin2006_3.pdf, p. 1.

[16] Ibid., p. 1.

[17] 29 C.F.R. §541.302 (July 1, 1990 ed.). DOL reached a similar conclusion from testimony provided at a hearing on February 2, 1971. The purpose of the hearing was to determine, among other things, the treatment of computer-related occupations under the exemption for executive, administrative, and professional employees. In response to testimony, DOL said "at the present time the computer sciences are not generally recognized by colleges and universities as a bona fide academic discipline with standardized licensing, certification, or registration procedures." U.S. Department of Labor, Wage and Hour Division, "Defining and Delimiting the Terms 'Any Employee Employed in a Bona Fide Executive, Administrative, or Professional Capacity (Including Any Employee Employed in the Capacity of Academic Administrative Personnel or Teacher in Elementary or Secondary Schools) or in the Capacity of Outside Salesman,'" Federal Register, vol. 36, December 2, 1971, p. 22977.

[18] 29 C.F.R. §541.118 (July 1, 1990 ed.).

[19] 29 C.F.R. §541.3 (July 1, 1990 ed.). According to regulations, time is an effective guide in determining an employee's primary duty. Primary duty "means the major part, or over 50 percent, of the employee's time." But, time alone may not be the sole test. Other factors may include the frequency with which an employee exercises discretion. 29 C.F.R. §541.103 (July 1, 1990 ed.).

[20] 29 C.F.R. §541.118 (July 1, 1990 ed.).

[21] The regulations that implemented the 1938 act defined a professional employee as someone whose job was predominantly intellectual in character, required educational training in a "specially organized body of knowledge," and involved the consistent exercise of discretion and judgment. Frank E. Cooper, "The Coverage of the Fair Labor Standards Act and Other Problems in Its Interpretation," Law and Contemporary Problems, Summer 1939, p. 348.

[22] U.S. Department of Labor, Wage and Hour Division, "Fair Labor Standard Act; Computer-Related Occupations; Exemption from Minimum Wage and Overtime Compensation Requirements; Final Rule," Federal Register, vol. 57, October 9, 1992, pp. 46742-46745.

[23] Ibid., p. 46743.

[24] The title of P.L. 104-188 (H.R. 3448) is the Small Business Job Protection Act of 1996.

[25] The minimum weekly salary of $455 may be paid in periods longer than a week (e.g., $910 biweekly or $1,971.66 a month); 29 C.F.R. §541.600(b). The $455 minimum weekly salary amount cannot include the value of employer-provided room or board; 29 C.F.R. §541.606. Professional employees may be exempt if they are paid on a fee, rather than a salary, basis. For example, an employee may be paid an agreed sum for a single job regardless of the time required to complete the job. To determine whether the fee payment meets the minimum amount of salary required for exemption, the fee must equal at least $455 per week if the employee worked 40 hours; 29 C.F.R. §541.605(a)-(b).

[26] The regulatory language for computer employees is now at 29 C.F.R. §§541.400-402. U.S. Department of Labor, Wage and Hour Division, "Defining and Delimiting the Exemptions for Executive, Administrative, Professional, Outside Sales and Computer Employees," Federal Register, vol. 69, April 23, 2004, p. 22267.

[27] According to the 2004 regulations, "The term 'primary duty' means the principal, main, major or most important duty that the employee performs.... Factors to consider when determining the primary duty of an employee include, but are not limited to, the relative importance of the exempt duties as compared with other types of duties; the amount of time spent performing exempt work; the employee's relative freedom from direct supervision; and the relationship between the employee's salary and the wages paid to other employees for the kind of nonexempt work performed by the employee"; 29 C.F.R. §541.700(a).

[28] 29 C.F.R. §541.400(a)-(b).

[29] Current regulations state "A job title alone is insufficient to establish the exempt status of an employee. The exempt or nonexempt status of any particular employee must be determined on the basis of whether the employee's salary and duties meet the requirements of the regulations in this part"; 29 CFR §541.2.

[30] 29 C.F.R. §541.401.

[31] The employer also asked if IT Support Specialists qualified for the administrative exemption under Section 13(a)(1). An employee may qualify for the administrative exemption if they are paid a salary of at least $455 a week and their primary duty "is the performance of office or non-manual work directly related to the management or general business operations of the employer or the employer's customers" and their primary duty "includes the exercise of discretion and independent judgment with respect to matters of significance"; 29. C.F.R. §541.200. WHD concluded that, based on the information presented by the employer, IT Support Specialists did not qualify for the administrative exemption. U.S. Department of Labor, Wage and Hour Division, Information Technology (IT) Support Specialist Under Sections 13(a)(1) and 13(a)(17), Opinion Letter FLSA2006-42, October 26, 2006, available at http://www.dol.gov/whd/opinion/ FLSA/2006/2006_10_26_42_FLSA.pdf, pp. 1-2, 5-6.

[32] 29 C.F.R. §541.3 (July 1, 1990 ed.).

In: The Fair Labor Standards Act …
Editor: Julian A. Sotelo
ISBN: 978-1-62808-301-9

Chapter 3

THE NATIONAL LABOR RELATIONS ACT: BACKGROUND AND SELECTED TOPICS*

Jon O. Shimabukuro

SUMMARY

The National Labor Relations Act (NLRA or "the Act") recognizes the right of employees to engage in collective bargaining through representatives of their own choosing. By "encouraging the practice and procedure of collective bargaining," the Act attempts to mitigate and eliminate labor-related obstructions to the free flow of commerce. Although union membership has declined dramatically since the 1950s, congressional interest in the NLRA remains significant. In the 112th Congress, over 30 bills have been introduced to amend the NLRA. Some of these bills address the timing of union representation elections, while others are concerned with varying aspects of the NLRA, such as the activities of the National Labor Relations Board (NLRB), which implements and administers the Act.

Since the NLRA's enactment in 1935, the NLRB and the courts have considered a variety of issues arising under the Act. This report reviews selected decisions of the NLRB and the courts on three of them. Determining when an employee may be deemed a supervisor for purposes of coverage under the Act is important because the right to engage in

* This is an edited, reformatted and augmented version of a Congressional Research Service publication, CRS Report for Congress R42703, from www.crs.gov, prepared for Members and Committees of Congress, dated September 7, 2012.

collective bargaining is extended only to employees under the NLRA. Employees who are properly classified as supervisors are not afforded collective bargaining rights.

Both employers and unions are prohibited from restraining or coercing employees in the exercise of the rights guaranteed to them under the Act. In general, to determine whether an unfair labor practice has been committed by either an employer or union, a reviewing court asks whether the misconduct "reasonably tends" to restrain or coerce employees in the exercise of their rights under the NLRA. Courts have emphasized that the actual effect of the misconduct is immaterial.

Finally, pre-election communication with employees may influence the outcome of a representation election. While the NLRA does prohibit an employer from interfering with an employee's collective bargaining rights, decisions discussed in this report indicate that an employer does not violate the Act in all cases when it denies a union access to its property.

INTRODUCTION

The National Labor Relations Act (NLRA or "the Act") recognizes the right of employees to engage in collective bargaining through representatives of their own choosing. By "encouraging the practice and procedure of collective bargaining," the Act attempts to mitigate and eliminate labor-related obstructions to the free flow of commerce.[1] Although union membership has declined dramatically since the 1950s, congressional interest in the NLRA remains significant.[2] In the 112th Congress, over 30 bills have been introduced to amend the NLRA. Some of these bills address the timing of union representation elections, while others are concerned with varying aspects of the NLRA, such as the activities of the National Labor Relations Board (NLRB), which implements and administers the Act. Since the NLRA's enactment in 1935, the NLRB and the courts have considered a variety of issues arising under the Act. This report reviews selected decisions of the NLRB and the courts that involve topics that continue to be relevant for employers and unions during the collective bargaining process.

COVERAGE UNDER THE NLRA

The right to engage in collective bargaining under the NLRA does not apply to all individuals employed by an employer.[3] Rather, the right extends only to "employees." Section 2(3) of the NLRA states that an employee "shall include any employee ... but shall not include any individual ... employed as a supervisor."[4] An employee's job title does not determine whether an individual is a supervisor for purposes of the NLRA. Instead, the term "supervisor" is defined by the Act to include any individual with the authority to perform any one of 12 specified functions, if the exercise of such authority requires the use of independent judgment and is not merely routine or clerical.

Section 2(11) of the NLRA states:

> The term "supervisor" means any individual having authority, in the interest of the employer, to hire, transfer, suspend, lay off, recall, promote, discharge, assign, reward, or discipline other employees, or responsibly to direct them, or to adjust their grievances, or effectively to recommend such action, if in connection with the foregoing the exercise of such authority is not of a merely routine or clerical nature, but requires the use of independent judgment.[5]

Because the 12 functions and the term "independent judgment" are not further defined, the NLRB and U.S. Supreme Court have sought to provide meaning to this language.

In *NLRB v. Kentucky River Community Care, Inc.*, the Court considered whether certain nurses should be classified as supervisors for purposes of the NLRA when their judgment was informed by professional or technical training or experience.[6] Kentucky River Community Care, the operator of a care facility for individuals with mental retardation and illness, sought to exclude six registered nurses (RNs) from a bargaining unit on the grounds that they were supervisors. The NLRB concluded that the nurses were not supervisors because they failed to exercise sufficient independent judgment. According to the NLRB, the nurses used "ordinary professional or technical judgment" in directing less-skilled employees to deliver services in accordance with employer-specified standards.[7] The U.S. Court of Appeals for the Sixth Circuit rejected the NLRB's position, and the Court ultimately affirmed the Sixth Circuit's decision.

The *Kentucky River* Court understood section 2(11) of the NLRA to set forth a three-part test for determining supervisory status. Employees will be considered supervisors if (1) they hold the authority to engage in any one of the twelve supervisory functions identified in section 2(11) of the NLRA; (2) their exercise of authority is not of a "merely routine or clerical nature, but requires the use of independent judgment," and (3) their authority is held in the interest of the employer.[8] At issue in *Kentucky River*, was the second part of the test. Although the Court recognized the NLRB's discretion to clarify the meaning of the term "independent judgment," it maintained that it was inappropriate for the NLRB to characterize judgment that reflects "ordinary professional or technical judgment" as failing to be independent judgment.

The Court believed that the NLRB's reference to "ordinary or technical judgment" established a "startling categorical exclusion" that was not suggested by the NLRA's statutory text.[9] The Court observed:

> What supervisory judgment worth exercising, one must wonder, does not rest on 'professional or technical skill or experience?' If the Board applied this aspect of its test to every exercise of a supervisory function, it would virtually eliminate 'supervisors' from the Act.[10]

In addition, the Court indicated that it was unaware of any NLRB decision that concluded that a supervisor's judgment ceased to be independent judgment because it depended on the supervisor's professional or technical training or experience.[11] The Court maintained that when an employee exercises one of the functions identified in section 2(11) with judgment that possesses a sufficient degree of independence, the NLRB "invariably finds supervisory status."[12]

Four justices dissented from the majority's position on independent judgment.[13] The dissent maintained that the NLRB's interpretation of independent judgment was fully rational and consistent with the NLRA. The dissent noted: "The term 'independent judgment' is indisputably ambiguous, and it is settled law that the NLRB's interpretation of ambiguous language in the [NLRA] is entitled to deference.[14]

In 2006, the NLRB revisited the issue of supervisory status in *Oakwood Healthcare, Inc.*[15] Oakwood Healthcare employed approximately 181 RNs in 10 patient care units at an acute care hospital. Many of these nurses served as charge nurses who were responsible for overseeing their patient care units and assigning other RNs, technicians, and medical personnel on their shifts. Some of the RNs worked permanently as charge nurses, while others rotated into the charge nurse position. Oakwood Healthcare sought to exclude both the permanent and the rotating charge nurses from a proposed bargaining unit on the grounds that they were supervisors within the meaning of section 2(11). Oakwood Healthcare maintained that the charge nurses were supervisors because they "used independent judgment in assigning and responsibly directing employees."[16]

The NLRB viewed *Oakwood Healthcare, Inc.* as an opportunity to define the terms "assign," "responsibly to direct," and "independent judgment" as they are used in section 2(11) of the NLRA.[17] With each term, the NLRB considered the language used by Congress, as well as the NLRA's legislative history, applicable policy considerations, and Supreme Court precedent.[18] The NLRB concluded that the term "assign" should be construed to refer to the act of designating an employee to a place (such as a location or department), appointing an employee to a time, or giving significant overall duties or tasks to an employee.[19] The NLRB noted that in the health care setting, the term "encompasses the charge nurses' responsibility to assign nurses and aides to particular patients."[20]

The term would not apply, however, to an individual who simply chooses the order in which an employee will perform discrete tasks within an assignment.

Citing the legislative history of section 2(11), the NLRB interpreted the term "responsibly to direct" to apply to individuals who not only oversee the work being performed, but are held responsible if the work is done poorly or not at all. The NLRB observed:

> [F]or direction to be 'responsible,' the person directing and performing the oversight of the employee must be accountable for the performance of the task by the other, such that some adverse consequence may befall the one providing the oversight if the tasks performed by the employee are not performed properly. This interpretation of 'responsibly to direct' is consistent with post-*Kentucky River* Board decisions that considered an accountability element for 'responsibly to direct.'[21]

According to the NLRB, to establish accountability for purposes of responsible direction, it must be shown that the employer delegated to the putative supervisor the authority to direct the work and the authority to take corrective action.[22] The possibility of adverse consequences for the putative supervisor must also be established.

With regard to the term "independent judgment," the NLRB maintained that at a minimum an individual must act or effectively recommend action that is "free of the control of others and form an opinion or evaluation by discerning and comparing data."[23] The NLRB further elaborated that a judgment is not independent if it is dictated or controlled by detailed instructions in company policies, the verbal instructions of a higher authority, or the provisions of a collective bargaining agreement.[24] The NLRB sought to interpret the term "independent judgment" in light of the phrase "not of a merely routine or clerical nature," which appears before "independent judgment" in section 2(11). The NLRB stated:

> If there is only one obvious and self-evident choice ... or if the assignment is made solely on the basis of equalizing workloads, then the assignment is routine or clerical in nature and does not implicate independent judgment, even if it is made free of the control of others and involves forming an opinion or evaluation by discerning and comparing data.[25]

Applying the new definitions for the terms "assign," "responsibly to direct," and "independent judgment," the NLRB concluded that 12 permanent charge nurses assigned to five of the 10 patient care units were supervisors for purposes of the NLRA.

The NLRB declined to find that any of the charge nurses responsibly directed other employees. The NLRB noted that the charge nurses were not subject to discipline or lower evaluations if employees who were subject to the nurses failed to adequately performed their tasks. However, in five of the 10 patient care units, the NLRB found that the charge nurses did assign employees within the meaning of the NLRA. These nurses assigned employees to patients and assigned overall tasks to the employees. The charge nurses in the five units were unlike emergency room charge nurses who simply placed staff in geographic areas within the emergency room.

The NLRB determined that the 12 charge nurses exercised independent judgment in accordance with section 2(11). The charge nurses made assignments in light of the skill sets of employees and the nursing time patients would require on a given shift. The NLRB noted that the "process of equalizing work loads at the hospital involves independent judgment."[26] While Oakwood Healthcare maintained a written policy for assigning nursing personnel to deliver care to patients, the NLRB observed that charge nurses were given considerable latitude in making decisions on how to assign nursing personnel.

Ultimately, the NLRB concluded that when a charge nurse makes an assignment based on the skill, experience, and temperament of nursing personnel and the patients, that nurse has "exercised the requisite discretion to make the assignment a supervisory function 'requir[ing] the use of independent judgment.'"[27]

UNFAIR LABOR PRACTICES AND INTERFERENCE WITH COLLECTIVE BARGAINING

In addition to recognizing the right of employees to engage in collective bargaining, the NLRA prohibits certain misconduct by both employers and unions that interferes with that right. Section 8(a)(1) of the Act states that it shall be an unfair labor practice for an employer to "interfere with, restrain, or coerce employees in the exercise of the rights guaranteed in section 7."[28] Similarly, section 8(b)(1)(A) of the NLRA provides that it shall be an unfair labor practice for a labor organization or its agents to "restrain or coerce ... employees in the exercise of the rights guaranteed in section 7 ..."[29]

Although the NLRB has suggested in the past that Congress did not intend for section 8(b)(1)(A) to be given the broad application sometimes accorded to section 8(a)(1), section 8(b)(1)(A) appears to be viewed generally as a counterpart to section 8(a)(1).[30] Indeed, in *Capital Service, Inc. v. NLRB*, a 1953 case involving a union boycott of goods manufactured by employees who resisted unionization, the U.S. Court of Appeals for the Ninth Circuit observed that it was "inconceivable" that the NLRA "intended the identical words 'restrain or coerce' of 8(a)(1) and 8(b)(1) to have a different meaning when applied to a labor organization from that when applied to an employer."[31]

To determine whether an unfair labor practice has been committed under either subsection, a reviewing court asks the same question: whether the misconduct "reasonably tends" to restrain or coerce employees in the exercise of their rights under the NLRA.[32] Courts have emphasized that the actual effect of the misconduct is immaterial. In *Int'l Union of Operating Engineers, AFL-CIO v. NLRB*, a 1964 case involving picketing and the right of employees to refrain from union activities, the Third Circuit maintained: "That no one was in fact coerced or intimidated is of no relevance. The test of coercion and intimidation is not whether the misconduct proves effective."[33]

Section 8(a)(1) of the NLRA prohibits not only the use or threatened use of violence against an employee for exercising his rights under section 7 of the Act, but also verbal threats to adversely affect an employee's employment status or working conditions.[34] In *NLRB v. Gissel Packing Co., Inc.*, the Supreme Court explained:

> [A]n employer is free to communicate to his employees any of his general views about unionism or any of his specific views about a particular union, so long as the communications do not contain a 'threat

> of reprisal or force or promise of benefit.' He may even make a prediction as to the precise effects he believes unionization will have on his company. In such a case, however, the prediction must be carefully phrased on the basis of objective fact to convey an employer's belief as to demonstrably probable consequences beyond his control or to convey a management decision already arrived at to close the plant in case of unionization.[35]

Whether an employer's communication to its employees constitutes an unlawful threat for purposes of section 8(a)(1) is generally fact-specific and requires consideration of the totality of the circumstances. The *Gissel* Court noted that any assessment of the precise scope of employer expression "must be made in the context of its labor relations setting" and must take into account the economic dependence of the employees on their employers.[36]

An employer's interrogation of its employees as to union sympathy and affiliation may also violate section 8(a)(1) of the Act because such an interrogation has a "natural tendency to instill in the minds of employees fear of discrimination on the basis of the information the employer has obtained."[37] In *Blue Flash Express, Inc.*, the NLRB indicated that it would consider five factors when determining whether an interrogation reasonably tends to restrain or interfere with the exercise of rights guaranteed by the NLRA: the timing of the interrogation; the place of the interrogation; the information sought during the interrogation; the identity of the interrogator; and the employer's conceded preference with respect to the subject of the interrogation.[38] Using these factors, the Board found a violation of section 8(a)(1) when an employer interrogated an employee after a performance review, despite resistance by the employee.[39] The Board also found a violation when an interrogation was conducted by a high-level supervisor, without a legitimate purpose, and without any assurances against reprisals.[40]

The use or threatened use of violence by a union or one of its agents is similarly considered an unfair labor practice under section 8(b)(1)(A) of the NLRA.[41] Other acts by unions have been found to violate section 8(b)(1)(A), including encouraging employees to quit their jobs because they were not members of the union, and threatening discharge for failure to sign union authorization cards.

In *Local Union No. 697 (UE & C Catalytic, Inc.)*, the NLRB found a violation of section 8(b)(1)(A) when a local union engaged in a pattern of misconduct to get members of other unions employed at an Amoco refinery, identified as "travelers," to abandon their jobs because they were not members of the local union and because a large number of local members were out of work.[42] The pattern of misconduct included repeated requests and suggestions that the travelers quit their jobs and volunteer for layoffs. The local also devised a credentialing system just for the travelers and refused to renew some of the credentials. The NLRB concluded that the local's efforts were coercive and meant to intimidate the travelers into leaving the refinery: "It wanted the travelers to leave the Amoco jobsite because they were not members of [the local] and because members were out of work."[43]

The NLRB has indicated that section 8(b)(1)(A) "broadly interdicts any union conduct threatening job security of employees because of the employees' refusal or failure to abide by union membership conditions."[44] By telling employees that they must sign a union authorization card or be subject to termination, a union makes "an implied threat of reprisal calculated to interfere with the employees' statutory right to refrain from any and all union activities."[45]

Unions have been found to violate section 8(b)(1)(A) by engaging in other misconduct, including attempting to cause an employer to discharge employees because they opposed the union leadership, refusing to refer dissident union members for jobs, and threatening employees with the loss of employment if they contested a union election.[46]

Pre-Election Communication with Employees

While section 8(a)(1) of the NLRA does prohibit an employer from interfering with the right of employees to engage in collective bargaining, the NLRB has long maintained that an employer may make antiunion, but noncoercive, speeches to their employees on company time and on company property without allowing a union an equal opportunity to reply. In *Livingston Shirt Corp.*, the NLRB noted:

> [W]e find nothing in the statute which even hints at any congressional intent to restrict an employer in the use of his own premises for the purpose of airing his views. On the contrary, an employer's premises are the natural forum for him just as the union hall is the inviolable forum for the union to assemble and address employees. We do not believe that unions will be unduly hindered in their right to carry on organizational activities by our refusal to open up to them the employer's premises for group meetings, particularly since this is an area from which they have traditionally been

excluded, and there remains open to them all the customary means for communicating with employees.[47]

Last-minute speeches made by employers, however, have been distinguished from other preelection speeches. In *Peerless Plywood Co.*, decided the same day as *Livingston Shirt*, the NLRB declared that employers and unions are prohibited from making election speeches on company time to massed assemblies of employees within 24 hours before an election.[48] The NLRB maintained that such speeches interfere with a free election by creating a "mass psychology which overrides arguments made through other campaign media and giv[ing] an unfair advantage to the party, whether employer or union, who in this manner obtains the last most telling word."[49]

In 1956, the Court considered whether an employer could prohibit the distribution of union literature on its company-owned parking lots by nonemployee union organizers. In *NLRB v. Babcock & Wilson Co.*, the employer contended that it had a consistent policy against all pamphleteering and that it was not attempting to impede its employees' collective bargaining rights when it restricted the distribution of union literature on company property. [50] The Court maintained an employer cannot be compelled to allow the distribution of union literature on its premises if a union can reach employees through other channels of communication. If, however, the employer's location and the employees' residences place the employees beyond the reach of reasonable union efforts to communicate with them, the employer must allow the union to approach its employees on its property. In *Babcock*, the Court ultimately found that the employer's restrictions were permissible because its plants were close to the communities where a large percentage of employees lived, and various methods of communication were available to the union.

In *Lechmere v. NLRB*, a 1992 case involving the efforts of the United Food and Commercial Workers Union, AFL-CIO, to organize employees at a retail store, the Court reaffirmed its holding in *Babcock*.[51] Rejecting the NLRB's conclusion that there were no reasonable, alternative means for the union to communicate with Lechmere's employees, the Court emphasized that *Babcock* requires access to an employer's property only when the employer's location and the employees' residences place the employees beyond the reach of reasonable union efforts to communicate with them. The Court identified logging camps, mining camps, and mountain resort hotels as "classic examples" where union access would be permitted.[52] The Court further noted that the union has the heavy burden of establishing employee isolation and showing that no other reasonable means of communicating with employees exists.[53] As in *Babcock*, the Court in *Lechmere* found that the union did have reasonable access to the retail employees and that this accessibility was suggested by the union's success in contacting a substantial percentage of them directly via mailings, phone calls, and home visits.[54]

End Notes

[1] See 29 U.S.C. § 151.

[2] See Bureau of Labor Statistics, U.S. Dept. of Labor, Union Members – 2011 (Jan. 27, 2012), available at http://www.bls.gov/news.release/pdf/union2.pdf (identifying the union membership rate for private sector workers in 2011 as 11.8 percent). See also Steven Greenhouse, Union Membership Rate Fell Again in 2011, N.Y. Times, Jan. 28, 2012, at B3 ("In the 1950s, more than 35 percent of private sector workers were in unions.").

[3] For additional information on coverage under the National Labor Relations Act, see CRS Report RL34350, The Definition of "Supervisor" Under the National Labor Relations Act, by Gerald Mayer and Jon O. Shimabukuro.

[4] 29 U.S.C. §152(3).

[5] 29 U.S.C. §152(11).

[6] 532 U.S. 706 (2001).

[7] Id. at 713.

[8] Id. (quoting 29 U.S.C. § 152(11)).

[9] Kentucky River Community Care, 532 U.S. at 714.

[10] Id. at 715.

[11] Id. at 716.

[12] Id.

[13] Justice Stevens filed an opinion, joined by Justices Souter, Ginsburg, and Breyer, that dissented from the majority opinion on the question of independent judgment. However, Justice Stevens' opinion concurred with the majority opinion on the question of which party bears the burden of proving or disproving an employee's supervisory status in an unfair labor practice proceeding.

[14] Kentucky River Community Care, 532 U.S. at 725-26.

[15] 348 NLRB 686 (2006).

[16] Id. at 687.

[17] Id. at 688 ("Thus, exercising our discretion to interpret ambiguous language in the Act, and consistent with the Supreme Court's instructions in Kentucky River, we herein adopt definitions for the terms 'assign,' 'responsibly to direct,' and 'independent judgment' as those terms are used in Section 2(11) of the Act.").

[18] See Oakwood Healthcare, 348 NLRB at 688-89.

[19] Oakwood Healthcare, 348 NLRB at 689.

[20] Id.

[21] Oakwood Healthcare, 348 NLRB at 691-92.

[22] Oakwood Healthcare, 348 NLRB at 692.

[23] Oakwood Healthcare, 348 NLRB at 693.

[24] Id. The NLRB did indicate that the mere existence of company policies would not eliminate independent judgment from decision-making if the policies allow for discretionary choices.

[25] Oakwood Healthcare, 348 NLRB at 693.

[26] Oakwood Healthcare, 348 NLRB at 697.

[27] Oakwood Healthcare, 348 NLRB at 698.

[28] 29 U.S.C. § 158(a)(1). Section 7 of the NLRA, 29 U.S.C. § 157, recognizes the right of employees to engage in collective bargaining.

[29] 29 U.S.C. § 158(b)(1)(A).

[30] See THE DEVELOPING LABOR LAW 90 (John E. Higgins et al. eds., 2006).

[31] 204 F.2d 848 (9th Cir. 1953), aff'd, 347 U.S. 501 (1954).

[32] Compare Presbyterian/St. Luke's Medical Center v. NLRB, 723 F.2d 1468, 1472 (10th Cir. 1983) ("The test for violations of section 8(a)(1) is not whether an attempt at coercion has succeeded or failed, but 'whether the employer engaged in conduct which reasonably tends to interfere with, restrain, or coerce employees in the free exercise of their section 7 rights.'"), and Local 542, Int'l Union of Operating Engineers, AFL-CIO v. NLRB, 328 F.2d 850, 852-53 (3rd Cir. 1964) ("The Union urges in support of its argument that the episodes 'had no effect upon the operation of the employer's business, and they coerced or intimidated no one.' ... The test is whether the misconduct is such that, under the circumstances existing, it may reasonably tend to coerce or intimidate employees in the exercise of rights protected under the Act.").

[33] Int'l Union of Operating Engineers, 328 F.2d at 852.

[34] See THE DEVELOPING LABOR LAW at 185-86 (discussing section 8(a)(1) of the NLRA and employer violence). See also Teamsters Local Union No. 171 v. NLRB, 863 F.2d 946, 952-53 (D.C. Cir. 1988) (describing various acts of misconduct that violate section 8(a)(1), including threatening to close a facility if employees select a union as their collective bargaining representative, and threatening to discharge employees for engaging in union activities).

[35] 395 U.S. 575, 618 (1969).

[36] Id. at 617.

[37] NLRB v. West Coast Casket Co., Inc., 205 F.2d 902, 904 (9th Cir. 1953).

[38] 109 NLRB 591 (1954).

[39] See Litton Systems, 300 NLRB 324 (1990).

[40] See North Hills Office Services, Inc., 344 NLRB 1083 (2005).

[41] See Teamsters Local 115 (Kurz-Hastings, Inc.), 344 NLRB 644 (2005). See also THE DEVELOPING LABOR LAW at 274-76 (discussing section 8(b)(1)(A) of the NLRA and employer violence).

[42] 318 NLRB 443 (1995).

[43] Id. at 446.

[44] United Stanford Employees, Local 680, 232 NLRB 326, 329 (1977).

[45] Id. See also Lockheed Martin Tactical Aircraft Systems, 331 NLRB 1407 (2000) (affirming Administrative Law Judge's finding that a union violated section 8(b)(1)(A) by telling employees who were reclassified into positions that fell within an existing bargaining unit that they would be discharged if they failed to sign authorization cards).

[46] See 1-5 Nat'l Lab. Rel. Act: Law & Prac. (MB) § 5.11.

[47] 107 NLRB 400, 406 (1953).

[48] 107 NLRB 427 (1953).

[49] Id. at 429.

[50] 351 U.S. 105 (1956).

[51] 502 U.S. 527 (1992).
[52] Id. at 539-40.
[53] Id. at 540.
[54] Id.

In: The Fair Labor Standards Act ... ISBN: 978-1-62808-301-9
Editor: Julian A. Sotelo

Chapter 4

THE DEFINITION OF "SUPERVISOR" UNDER THE NATIONAL LABOR RELATIONS ACT*

Gerald Mayer and Jon O. Shimabukuro

SUMMARY

The National Labor Relations Act (NLRA) establishes certain protections for private sector employees who want to form or join a labor union. These protections do not extend to supervisors. Historically, Congress has debated where to draw the line between employees who have different levels of management responsibility. It is generally agreed that employees who have significant supervisory duties, such as hiring and firing, are supervisors. However, disagreement occurs with respect to employees who have minor supervisory duties.

In 2001, the U.S. Supreme Court ruled that the test administered by the National Labor Relations Board ("NLRB" or the "Board") to determine whether an employee is a supervisor was inconsistent with the NLRA. In response to *NLRB v. Kentucky River Community Care, Inc.*, the Board issued a September 2006 decision in *Oakwood Healthcare, Inc.* in which it established new definitions for three key terms that are used to identify supervisors for purposes of the NLRA: to "assign" and

---

* This is an edited, reformatted and augmented version of a Congressional Research Service publication, CRS Report for Congress RL34350, from www.crs.gov, prepared for Members and Committees of Congress, dated July 5, 2012.

"responsibly to direct" employees and to exercise "independent judgment."

Applying the new definitions, the NLRB concluded that 12 permanent charge nurses employed by Oakwood Healthcare were supervisors. The Board found that the nurses exercised independent judgment in assigning employees to patients and assigning overall tasks to other employees. However, the Board found that none of the charge nurses at Oakwood Healthcare responsibly directed other employees.

In the 112th Congress, Senator Richard Blumenthal introduced the Re-Empowerment of Skilled and Professional Employees and Construction Tradesworkers (RESPECT) Act (S. 2168). The legislation was also introduced in the 110th Congress by Representative Robert Andrews and Senator Chris Dodd (H.R. 1644/S. 969).

The RESPECT Act would narrow the definition of the term "supervisor" in the NLRA. The legislation would eliminate "assign" and "responsibly to direct" from the current definition of supervisor in the NLRA. In addition, the act would add a limiting phrase to the definition of supervisor. Under the act, employees would be classified as supervisors if they are engaged in supervisory activities more than 50% of the time. Currently, an employee may be classified as a supervisor if the employee acts as a supervisor for at least 10%-15% of the employee's worktime. This change would reduce the number of employees who are classified as supervisors and, therefore, increase the number of employees protected by the NLRA.

The RESPECT Act, if it were enacted, may have a significant impact on foremen. In 1947, the Supreme Court upheld the position that the Board followed at the time that supervisors were included in the definition of employee. In response, Congress amended the NLRA to exclude supervisors from the definition of employee. The new definition was included in the Labor Management Relations Act of 1947 (P.L. 80-101). Because the RESPECT Act would eliminate "responsibly to direct" as a supervisory function, foremen and employees with similar duties may no longer be classified as supervisors. They could, therefore, receive the same protections as other employees under the NLRA.

INTRODUCTION

The National Labor Relations Act (NLRA) establishes certain protections for private sector employees who want to form or join a labor union. These protections do not extend to supervisors. Historically, Congress has debated where to draw the line between employees who have different levels of management responsibility. It is generally agreed that employees who have significant supervisory duties, such as hiring and firing, are supervisors. However, disagreement occurs with respect to employees who have minor supervisory duties.

In 2001, the U.S. Supreme Court ruled that the test administered by the National Labor Relations Board (hereinafter referred to as the "NLRB" or the "Board") to determine whether an employee is a supervisor was inconsistent with the NLRA.[1] In response to *NLRB v. Kentucky River Community Care, Inc.*, the Board issued a decision in September 2006 in *Oakwood Healthcare, Inc.* in which it established new definitions for key terms that are used to identify supervisors under the NLRA.

In the 112th Congress, Senator Richard Blumenthal introduced the Re-Empowerment of Skilled and Professional Employees and Construction Tradesworkers (RESPECT) Act (S. 2168). The legislation would narrow the definition of the term "supervisor" in the NLRA. The RESPECT Act was introduced in the 110th Congress by Representative Robert Andrews and Senator Chris Dodd (H.R. 1644/S. 969).

This report examines the potential impact of the RESPECT Act in terms of the NLRB's decision in *Oakwood Healthcare, Inc.* The report begins with the definitions of "employee" and "supervisor" under the NLRA. Next, it examines the decision in *Oakwood Healthcare, Inc.* The report then summarizes the RESPECT Act and examines its potential impact on the number of employees protected by the NLRA.

THE DEFINITION OF EMPLOYEE UNDER THE NLRA

Section 7 of the NLRA identifies the collective bargaining rights of most employees in the private sector. Section 7 provides, in relevant part:

> Employees shall have the right to self-organization, to form, join, or assist labor organizations, to bargain collectively through representatives of their own choosing ... and shall also have the right to refrain from any or all of such activities.[2]

Section 2(3) of the act states that an employee "shall include any employee ... but shall not include any individual ... employed as a supervisor."[3] An employee's job title does not determine whether the employee is a supervisor.[4] Rather, the term "supervisor" is defined to include any individual with the authority to perform any one of 12 specified functions, if the exercise of such authority requires the use of independent judgment and is not merely routine or clerical.

According to section 2(11) of the NLRA:

> The term "supervisor" means any individual having authority, in the interest of the employer, to hire, transfer, suspend, lay off, recall, promote, discharge, assign, reward, or discipline other employees, or responsibly to direct them, or to adjust their grievances, or effectively to recommend such action, if in connection with the foregoing the exercise of such authority is not of a merely routine or clerical nature, but requires the use of independent judgment.[5]

Because the 12 functions and the term "independent judgment" are not further defined, the NLRB and Supreme Court have sought to provide meaning to this language.

THE KENTUCKY RIVER CASE AND OAKWOOD HEALTHCARE, INC.

In *NLRB v. Kentucky River Community Care, Inc.*, the U.S. Supreme Court considered whether certain nurses should be classified as supervisors for purposes of the NLRA when their judgment was based on professional or technical training or experience. Kentucky River Community Care, the operator of a care facility for individuals with mental retardation and illness, sought to exclude six registered nurses from a bargaining unit on the grounds that they were supervisors. The NLRB concluded that the nurses were not supervisors because they failed to exercise sufficient independent judgment. According to the Board, the nurses used "ordinary professional or technical judgment" in directing less-skilled employees to deliver services in accordance with employer-specified standards.[6] The U.S. Court of Appeals for the Sixth Circuit rejected the Board's position, and the Supreme Court affirmed the Sixth Circuit's decision.

The *Kentucky River* Court understood section 2(11) of the NLRA to set forth a three-part test for determining supervisory status. Employees will be considered supervisors if (1) they hold the authority to engage in any one of the 12 supervisory functions identified in section 2(11); (2) their exercise of authority is not of a "merely routine or clerical nature, but requires the use of independent judgment," and (3) their authority is held in the interest of the employer.[7] At issue in *Kentucky River* was the second part of the test. Although the Court recognized the NLRB's discretion to clarify the meaning of the term "independent judgment," it maintained that it was inappropriate for the Board to characterize judgment that reflects "ordinary professional or technical judgment" as failing to be independent judgment.

The Court said that the NLRB's reference to "ordinary professional or technical judgment" established a "startling categorical exclusion" that was not suggested by the statutory text of the NLRA.[8] The Court observed:

> What supervisory judgment worth exercising, one must wonder, does not rest on 'professional or technical skill or experience?' If the Board applied this aspect of its test to every exercise of a supervisory function, it would virtually eliminate 'supervisors' from the Act.[9]

Moreover, the Court indicated that it was unaware of any NLRB decision that concluded that a supervisor's judgment ceased to be independent judgment because it depended on the supervisor's professional or technical training or experience.[10] The Court maintained that when an employee exercises one of the functions identified in section 2(11) with judgment that possesses a sufficient degree of independence, the NLRB "invariably finds supervisory status."[11]

Four justices dissented from the majority's position on independent judgment.[12] The dissent maintained that the NLRB's interpretation of independent judgment was fully rational and consistent with the NLRA. The dissent noted: "The term 'independent judgment' is indisputably ambiguous, and it is settled law that the NLRB's interpretation of ambiguous language in the [NLRA] is entitled to deference."[13]

In September 2006, the NLRB revisited the issue of supervisory status in *Oakwood Healthcare, Inc.*[14] Oakwood Healthcare employed approximately 181 registered nurses (RNs) in 10 patient care units at an acute care hospital. Many of the nurses served as charge nurses who were responsible for overseeing their patient care units and assigning other RNs, technicians, and medical personnel on their shifts. Some of the RNs worked permanently as charge nurses, while others rotated into the charge nurse position. Oakwood Healthcare sought to exclude both the permanent and the rotating charge nurses from a proposed bargaining unit on the grounds that the nurses were supervisors within the meaning of section 2(11). Oakwood Healthcare maintained that the charge nurses were supervisors because they "used independent judgment in assigning and responsibly directing employees."[15]

The NLRB viewed *Oakwood Healthcare, Inc.* as an opportunity to define the terms "assign," "responsibly to direct," and "independent judgment" as those terms are used in section 2(11) of the NLRA.[16] For each term, the NLRB considered the language used by Congress, as well as the NLRA's legislative history, applicable policy considerations, and Supreme Court precedent.[17] The NLRB concluded that the term "assign" should be construed to refer to the act of designating an employee to a place (such as a location or department), appointing an employee to a time, or giving significant overall duties or tasks to an employee.[18] The NLRB noted that in the health care setting, the term "encompasses the charge nurses' responsibility to assign nurses and aides to particular patients."[19] The term would not apply, however, to an individual who simply chooses the order in which an employee will perform discrete tasks within an assignment.

Citing the legislative history of section 2(11), the NLRB interpreted the term "responsibly to direct" to apply to individuals who not only oversee the work being performed, but are held responsible if the work is done poorly or not at all. The NLRB observed:

> for direction to be 'responsible,' the person directing and performing the oversight of the employee must be accountable for the performance of the task by the other, such that some adverse consequence may befall the one providing the oversight if the tasks performed by the employee are not performed properly. This interpretation of 'responsibly to direct' is consistent with post-*Kentucky River* Board decisions that considered an accountability element for 'responsibly to direct.'[20]

According to the Board, to establish accountability for purposes of responsible direction, it must be shown that the employer delegated to the putative supervisor the authority to direct the work and the authority to take corrective action.[21]

The possibility of adverse consequences for the putative supervisor must also be established.

With regard to the term "independent judgment," the NLRB maintained that at a minimum an individual must act or effectively recommend action that is "free of the control of others and form an opinion or evaluation by discerning and comparing data."[22] The Board further elaborated that a judgment is not independent if it is dictated or controlled by detailed instructions in company policies, the verbal instructions of a higher authority, or the provisions of a collective bargaining agreement.[23]

The NLRB sought to interpret the term "independent judgment" in light of the phrase "not of a merely routine or clerical nature," which appears before "independent judgment" in section 2(11). The NLRB stated:

> If there is only one obvious and self-evident choice ... or if the assignment is made solely on the basis of equalizing workloads, then the assignment is routine or clerical in nature and does not implicate independent judgment.[24]

Applying the new definitions for the terms "assign," "responsibly to direct," and "independent judgment," the NLRB concluded that 12 permanent charge nurses employed in 5 of 10 patient care units at Oakwood Healthcare were supervisors for purposes of the NLRA.[25] Within the new meaning of the terms:

- *Assign.* The Board found that 12 charge nurses assigned employees to patients and assigned overall tasks to other employees.
- *Responsibly to Direct.* The Board did not find that any of the charge nurses at Oakwood Healthcare responsibly directed other employees. The Board concluded that the charge nurses were not subject to discipline or lower evaluations if employees they directed failed to adequately perform their tasks.
- *Independent Judgment.* Finally, the Board found that the 12 charge nurses exercised independent judgment in assigning other staff. The charge nurses made assignments in light of the skills of employees and the nursing time that would be required during a given shift. The NLRB noted that the "process of equalizing work loads at the hospital involves independent judgment."[26] Although Oakwood Healthcare maintained a written policy for assigning nursing personnel to deliver care to patients, the Board observed that charge nurses were given considerable latitude in making decisions on how to assign nursing personnel.

  The Board concluded that when a charge nurse makes an assignment based on the skill, experience, and temperament of nursing personnel and the patients, that nurse has "exercised the requisite discretion to make the assignment a supervisory function 'requir[ing] the use of independent judgment'."[27]

In addition, the Board found that, because the 12 charge nurses served in that capacity on every shift that they worked, they spent a "regular and substantial" portion of their work time performing supervisory functions.

The Board also found that charge nurses in the emergency room were not supervisors. The Board concluded that the nurses did not exercise independent judgment in assigning employees to places within the emergency room.

Finally, the Board found that none of the rotating charge nurses was a supervisor.

Dissent in Oakwood Healthcare, Inc.

The dissent in *Oakwood Healthcare, Inc.* maintained that the definitions established by the NLRB would have the effect of removing collective bargaining rights from many employees with only minor supervisory responsibilities.

The dissent noted that the language of the NLRA, its structure, and its legislative history "all point to significantly narrower interpretations of the ambiguous statutory terms 'assign ... other employees' and 'responsibly to direct them' than the majority adopts."[28]

The dissent was especially critical of the majority's definition of the term "assign." By defining the term to include the assignment of tasks, the dissent said that the majority disregarded the syntax of section 2(11), which states, in relevant part: "

The term 'supervisor' means any individual having authority, in the interest of the employer, to ... assign ... other employees." Citing *Kentucky River*, the dissent noted that the word "employees" serves as the grammatical object of the verbs identifying supervisory functions in section 2(11). The dissent stated simply: "In short, it must be the employees who are being assigned, not the tasks."[29]

The dissent also challenged the majority's definition of the term "responsibly to direct." Citing the legislative history of the term, the dissent maintained that the term refers to the "general supervisory authority delegated to foremen overseeing an operational department and the accountability that goes with it, in contrast to the kind of one-on-one task direction" that would be given to an employee.[30]

The dissent noted that the majority's definition failed to recognize the "scope and scale of supervisory function that 'responsibly to direct' was intended to capture."[31]

THE RESPECT ACT

In the 110th Congress, following the decision in *Oakwood Healthcare Inc.*, Representative Robert Andrews and Senator Chris Dodd introduced the Re-Empowerment of Skilled and Professional Employees and Construction Tradesworkers (RESPECT) Act (H.R. 1644/S. 969).[32] The legislation was not introduced in the 111th Congress. The RESPECT Act was introduced in the 112th Congress by Senator Richard Blumenthal (S. 2128).

The RESPECT Act would create a narrower definition of supervisor than exists under current law. Supporters of the legislation argue that the RESPECT Act would ensure that only true supervisors are excluded from protection under the NLRA.[33] Opponents maintain that the legislation would change the definition of supervisor that has been in place for 60 years.[34]

The RESPECT Act would amend the NLRA's definition of "supervisor" by removing two supervisory functions from the existing 12 functions and by adding a limiting phrase. The legislation would eliminate "assign" and "responsibly to direct" from the current supervisory functions.[35] In addition, the act would add (immediately after "in the interest of the employer") the phrase "and for a majority of the individual's worktime." This addition would seem to respond to the NLRB's decision in *Oakwood Healthcare, Inc.* In its decision, the Board maintained:

> Where an individual is engaged part time as a supervisor and the rest of the time as a unit employee, the legal standard for a supervisory determination is whether the individual spends a regular and substantial portion of his/her work time performing supervisory functions. Under the Board's standard, "regular" means according to a pattern or schedule, as opposed to sporadic substitution. The Board has not adopted a strict numerical definition of substantial and has found supervisory status where the individuals have served in a supervisory role for at least 10-15 percent of their total work time. We find no reason to depart from this established precedent.[36]

Under the RESPECT Act, an employee would be classified as a supervisor if he or she was engaged in supervisory activities at least 50% of the time.

The RESPECT Act would not apply to railroad or airline employees. Workers in both industries are covered by the Railway Labor Act. Nor would the legislation apply to most federal employees, who are covered by Federal Labor-Management Labor Relations Statute.

POTENTIAL IMPACT OF THE RESPECT ACT

The RESPECT Act would create a more restrictive definition of supervisor than exists since the decision in *Oakwood Healthcare, Inc.* The measure would reduce the number of supervisory functions from 12 to 10. For a larger employer, many of the remaining functions (e.g., hiring, firing, or transferring) may be performed by a human resource department. Because the act would eliminate "responsibly to direct" as a supervisory function, foremen and employees with similar duties may no longer be classified as supervisors.

Under current law, an employee may be classified as a supervisor if the employee performs supervisory functions at least 10%-15% of the employee's worktime. The RESPECT Act would raise this threshold to anything more than 50%. Even if the functions "assign" and "responsibly to direct" were not removed from the current definition of supervisor, this change would reduce the number of employees who are classified as supervisors. Because they would be included in the definition of employee, they would receive the protections provided by the NLRA.

Foremen

The RESPECT Act may have a significant effect on foremen and employees with similar duties. In 1947, the Supreme Court upheld the position that the Board followed at the time that supervisors were included in the definition of employee. In response, Congress amended the NLRA to exclude supervisors from the definition of employee. The new definition was included in the Labor Management Relations Act of 1947 (P.L. 80-101), commonly called the Taft-Hartley Act after its main sponsors Robert Taft and Fred Hartley Jr.

The House report on legislation approved in the House said that the legislation excluded "foremen and other supervisory personnel from the definition of 'employee.'" In the Senate, Senator Ralph Flanders offered an amendment to add "responsibly to direct" to a list of 11 supervisory functions that were in the Senate bill. Senator Flanders said:

> The definition of "supervisor" in this act seems to cover adequately everything except the basic act of supervising. Many of the activities described in [section 2(11)] are transferred in modern practice to a personnel manager or department.... In fact, under some modern

> management methods, the supervisor might be deprived of authority for most of the functions enumerated.... He is charged with the responsible direction of his department and the men under him. He determines under general orders what job shall be undertaken next and who shall do it. He gives instructions for its proper performance.

The Senate report on its version of the Labor Management Relations Act said that the amended definition of employee distinguishes "between straw bosses, leadmen, set-up men, and other minor supervisory employees, on the one hand, and the supervisor vested with such genuine management prerogatives as the right to hire or fire, discipline, or make effective recommendations with respect to such action." The Report went on to say that, without the change in definition, "management would be deprived of the undivided loyalty of its foremen."[37]

By eliminating the function "responsibly to direct" employees from the definition of supervisor, the RESPECT Act may increase the number of employees protected by the NLRA.

ESTIMATING THE IMPACT OF OAKWOOD HEALTHCARE, INC. AND THE RESPECT ACT

Regardless of how the decision in *Oakwood Healthcare, Inc.* is applied, it is difficult to estimate how many employees may be affected. Similarly, it is difficult to estimate how many employees may be affected by the RESPECT Act, if it were enacted. Data from household and employer surveys that are often used to estimate the potential impact of policy changes may not include enough information to identify whether an employee is a supervisor under the NLRA. For example, a person's occupation or job title may not be sufficient to determine whether an employee should be classified as a supervisor. Equally important, surveys usually do not ask respondents how much time they spend on different tasks—information that would be needed to determine the percentage of time that an employee spends on supervisory activities.

Nevertheless, removing the phrase "responsibly to direct" from the definition of supervisor may result in many foremen and similar workers being reclassified as employees for purposes of collective bargaining. A 2002 report by the Government Accountability Office (GAO) estimated that, in February 2001, there were an estimated 8.6 million full-time foremen in the private sector who were not covered by the NLRA. In the GAO report, foremen are "first-line" supervisors.[38]

Using data from the Current Population Survey (CPS), in 2011, there were an estimated 6.8 million full-time, first-line supervisors in the private sector. If part-time employees are included, there were an estimated 7.4 million first-line supervisors in the private sector in 2011.[39] Because of the slow economic recovery following the 2007-2009 recession, the number of private sector jobs in 2011 was below the number in 2001 (109.3 million in 2011 versus 110.7 million in 2001).[40]

According to an estimate by the Economic Policy Institute, if Oakwood Healthcare's interpretation of the definition of supervisor were to stand (i.e., applying the definition of supervisor to all charge nurses, including rotating charge nurses), 8 million workers would no longer be protected by the NLRA.[41] In the *Oakwood Healthcare, Inc.* decision, however, the NLRB concluded that 12 permanent charge nurses were supervisors and that none of the rotating charge nurses was a supervisor. In the two other decisions announced on the same day, the Board concluded that, in *Croft Metals*, none of approximately 25-35 lead persons were supervisors.[42] And in *Golden Crest Healthcare*, the Board decided that none of 19 nurses was a supervisor.

End Notes

[1] NLRB v. Kentucky River Community Care, Inc., 532 U.S. 706 (2001).
[2] 29 U.S.C. § 157.
[3] 29 U.S.C. § 152(3).
[4] For example, see Frenchtown Acquisition Co. v. NLRB, 6th Circuit, Nos. 11-1418/1499, June 20, 2012, p. 6.
[5] 29 U.S.C. § 152(11).
[6] 532 U.S. at 713.
[7] Id (quoting 29 U.S.C. § 152(11)).
[8] 532 U.S. at 714.
[9] 532 U.S. at 715.
[10] 532 U.S. at 716.
[11] Id.
[12] Justice Stevens filed an opinion, joined by Justices Souter, Ginsburg, and Breyer, that dissented from the majority opinion on the question of independent judgment. However, Justice Stevens' opinion concurred with the majority opinion on the question of which party bears the burden of proving or disproving an employee's supervisory status in an unfair labor practice proceeding.
[13] 532 U.S. at 725-726.
[14] 348 NLRB No. 37 (2006).
[15] Id. at 2.

[16] 348 NLRB at 3 ("Thus, exercising our discretion to interpret ambiguous language in the Act, and consistent with the Supreme Court's instructions in Kentucky River, we herein adopt definitions for the terms 'assign,' 'responsibly to direct,' and 'independent judgment' as those terms are used in Section 2(11) of the Act.").

[17] See 348 NLRB at 4.

[18] Id.

[19] Id.

[20] 348 NLRB at 8.

[21] Id.

[22] 348 NLRB at 9.

[23] 348 NLRB at 10. The NLRB did indicate, however, that the mere existence of company policies would not eliminate independent judgment from decision-making if the policies allow for discretionary choices.

[24] 348 NLRB at 8-9.

[25] In two other decisions issued on the same day as Oakwood Healthcare, Inc., the NLRB applied its new definitions and concluded that charge nurses at a nursing home in Hibbing, MN, and so-called "lead persons" at a manufacturing facility in McComb, MS, were not supervisors. See Beverly Enterprises-Minnesota, Inc., d/b/a/ Golden Crest Healthcare Center, 348 NLRB No. 39 (2006); Croft Metals, Inc., 348 NLRB No. 38 (2006).

[26] 348 NLRB at 16.

[27] Id.

[28] 348 NLRB at 20.

[29] 348 NLRB at 24.

[30] 348 NLRB at 28.

[31] Id.

[32] On May 8, 2007, the House Education and Labor Subcommittee on Health, Employment, Labor, and Pensions held a hearing on the RESPECT Act. On September 19, 2007, the full committee approved the measure by a vote of 26 to 20. The Senate did not consider the legislation.

[33] Honorable George Miller, Markup of H.R. 1644, The Re-Empowerment of Skilled and Professional Employees and Construction Tradesworkers (RESPECT) Act, opening statement, September 19, 2007, p. 2.

[34] Honorable Howard P. "Buck" McKeon, Markup of H.R. 1644, Re-Empowerment of Skilled and Professional Employees and Construction Tradesworkers (RESPECT) Act, press release, September 19, 2007, p. 1.

[35] As introduced in the 110th Congress, H.R. 1644 provided for the elimination of the clause "responsibility to direct them" from the NLRA's definition of the term "supervisor." During consideration of H.R. 1644 by the House Committee on Education and Labor, the language was corrected to provide for the elimination of the clause "responsibly to direct them." S. 2168, from the 112th Congress, would also eliminate the phrase "responsibly to direct them."

[36] 348 NLRB at 11.

[37] National Labor Relations Board, Legislative History of the Labor Management Relations Act, 1947, Washington: U.S. Govt. Print. Off., 1985, pp. 304, 410-411, 1303.

[38] "First-line" supervisors are employees who direct staff in face-to-face meetings (instead of through an intermediate supervisor) and who do not have as their principal duty the same work as their subordinates. U.S. Government Accountability Office, Collective Bargaining

Rights: Information on the Number of Workers With and Without Bargaining Rights, GAO-02-835, September 2002, pp. 12, 30-31.

[39] Calculated by CRS from the monthly Current Population Survey (CPS). The CPS is the source of the monthly national unemployment rate and other labor market information.

[40] The economic recession that began in the United States in December 2007 officially ended in June 2009. (National Bureau of Economic Research, U.S. Business Cycle Expansions and Contractions, http://www.nber.org/cycles/ cyclesmain.html.) U.S. Department of Labor, Bureau of Labor Statistics, Current Employment Statistics, http://stats.bls.gov/ces/.

[41] Ross Eisenbrey and Lawrence Mishel, Supervisor in Name Only: Union Rights of Eight Million Workers at Stake in Labor Board Ruling, Issue Brief 225, July 12, 2006, available at http://www.epinet.org/issuebriefs/225/ib225.pdf, pp. 1-2.

[42] See note 25.

INDEX

A

B

C

G

H

I

J

L

M

N

O

P